DEADLY DISEASES AND EPIDEMICS

WEST NILE VIRUS

Second Edition

DEADLY DISEASES AND EPIDEMICS

DEADLY DISEASES AND EPIDEMICS

WEST NILE VIRUS

Second Edition

Jeffrey Sfakianos
and Alan Hecht, D.C.

CONSULTING EDITOR
Hilary Babcock, M.D., M.P.H.,
Infectious Diseases Division,
Washington University School of Medicine,
Medical Director of Occupational Health (Infectious Diseases),
Barnes-Jewish Hospital and St. Louis Children's Hospital

FOREWORD BY
David Heymann
World Health Organization

CHELSEA HOUSE
PUBLISHERS
An imprint of Infobase Publishing

Chelsea House
An imprint of Infobase Publishing
132 West 31st Street
New York NY 10001

Library of Congress Cataloging-in-Publication Data

Sfakianos, Jeffrey N.
  West nile virus / Jeffrey Sfakianos and Alan Hecht ; consulting editor, Hilary Babcock; foreword by David Heymann. — 2nd ed.
      p. cm. — (Deadly diseases and epidemics)
  Includes bibliographical references and index.
  ISBN-13: 978-1-60413-254-0 (hardcover : alk. paper)
  ISBN-10: 1-60413-254-X (hardcover : alk. paper) 1. West Nile fever. 2. West Nile virus. I. Hecht, Alan. II. Babcock, Hilary. III. Title. IV. Series.

  RA644.W47S46 2009
  614.5'8856—dc22
                                   2009031055

Chelsea House books are available at special discounts when purchased in bulk quantities for businesses, associations, institutions, or sales promotions. Please call our Special Sales Department in New York at (212) 967-8800 or (800) 322-8755.

You can find Chelsea House on the World Wide Web at http://www.chelseahouse.com

Text design by Terry Mallon
Illustrations by Dale Williams
Cover design by Takeshi Takahashi
Composition by Mary Susan Ryan-Flynn
Cover printed by Bang Printing, Brainerd, MN
Book printed and bound by Bang Printing, Brainerd, MN.
Date printed: November 2009
Printed in the United States of America

10 9 8 7 6 5 4 3 2 1

This book is printed on acid-free paper.

All links and Web addresses were checked and verified to be correct at the time of publication. Because of the dynamic nature of the Web, some addresses and links may have changed since publication and may no longer be valid.

Table of Contents

Foreword

Communicable diseases kill and cause long-term disability. The microbial agents that cause them are dynamic, changeable, and resilient: They are responsible for more than 14 million deaths each year, mainly in developing countries.

Approximately 46 percent of all deaths in the developing world are due to communicable diseases, and almost 90 percent of these deaths are from AIDS, tuberculosis, malaria, and acute diarrheal and respiratory infections of children. In addition to causing great human suffering, these high-mortality communicable diseases have become major obstacles to economic development. They are a challenge to control either because of the lack of effective vaccines, or because the drugs that are used to treat them are becoming less effective because of antimicrobial drug resistance.

Millions of people, especially those who are poor and living in developing countries, are also at risk from disabling communicable diseases such as polio, leprosy, lymphatic filariasis, and onchocerciasis. In addition to human suffering and permanent disability, these communicable diseases create an economic burden—both on the workforce that handicapped persons are unable to join, and on their families and society, upon which they must often depend for economic support.

Finally, the entire world is at risk of the unexpected communicable diseases, those that are called emerging or re-emerging infections. Infection is often unpredictable because risk factors for transmission are not understood, or because it often results from organisms that cross the species barrier from animals to humans. The cause is often viral, such as Ebola and Marburg hemorrhagic fevers and severe acute respiratory syndrome (SARS). In addition to causing human suffering and death, these infections place health workers at great risk and are costly to economies. Infections such as Bovine Spongiform Encephalopathy (BSE) and the associated new human variant of Creutzfeldt-Jakob disease (vCJD) in Europe, and avian influenza A (H5N1) in Asia, are reminders of the seriousness of emerging and re-emerging infections. In addition, many of these infections have the potential to cause pandemics, which are a constant threat to our economies and public health security.

Science has given us vaccines and anti-infective drugs that have helped keep infectious diseases under control. Nothing demonstrates the effectiveness of vaccines better than the successful eradication of smallpox, the decrease in polio as the eradication program continues, and the decrease in measles when routine immunization programs are supplemented by mass vaccination campaigns.

Likewise, the effectiveness of anti-infective drugs is clearly demonstrated through prolonged life or better health in those infected with viral diseases such as AIDS, parasitic infections such as malaria, and bacterial infections such as tuberculosis and pneumococcal pneumonia.

But current research and development is not filling the pipeline for new anti-infective drugs as rapidly as resistance is developing, nor is vaccine development providing vaccines for some of the most common and lethal communicable diseases. At the same time, providing people with access to existing anti-infective drugs, vaccines, and goods such as condoms or bed nets—necessary for the control of communicable diseases in many developing countries—remains a great challenge.

Education, experimentation, and the discoveries that grow from them are the tools needed to combat high mortality infectious diseases, diseases that cause disability, or emerging and re-emerging infectious diseases. At the same time, partnerships between developing and industrialized countries can overcome many of the challenges of access to goods and technologies. This book may inspire its readers to set out on the path of drug and vaccine development, or on the path to discovering better public health technologies by applying our current understanding of the human genome and those of various infectious agents. Readers may likewise be inspired to help ensure wider access to those protective goods and technologies. Such inspiration, with pragmatic action, will keep us on the winning side of the struggle against communicable diseases.

David L. Heymann
Assistant Director General
Health Security and Environment
Representative of the Director General for Polio Eradication
World Health Organization
Geneva, Switzerland

1

The West Nile Panic

After a day of waterskiing at the lake, a group of friends and family members in suburban New York gathered around the grill, cooking hot dogs and hamburgers, and swimming in the pool. Everyone was enjoying the last days of summer break before the new school year began. The grandparents had traveled from Georgia to New York so they could be there when their grandson began his first day of elementary school.

It seemed like the perfect weekend. The sky was blue, the weather was still warm, and there was not an obvious worry anywhere in sight. As the sun set on that Saturday, the friends left for their own homes, and the family began to clean the plates and pool supplies from the backyard.

While the mother was cleaning up some used towels, she noticed a dead blue jay near the pool house. Although she was startled at first, she instinctively realized that the dead bird could not harm her, so she asked her husband to dispose of the bird's body. Nobody questioned what might have killed the bird. It was not all that unusual to see a dead bird when you spend a lot of time outdoors as the family had been doing that summer.

Later that evening, as the grandparents were telling their grandson a bedtime story about their own first days of school, the grandmother scratched a mosquito bite on her arm. Much like the dead bird, the mosquito bite did not get much attention from the family. After all, everyone has had a mosquito bite at some time or another; the bite itches for a few days and then it goes away.

On Monday morning, the grandmother felt very tired and suspected that she had not fully recovered from the busy weekend. After lunch she took a nap, hoping to wake up feeling more energetic. The family had plans to go shopping for school clothes that afternoon, and she wanted to make sure she felt well enough to go with them. However, when she woke up, she felt even worse. She had a headache and a fever. The family decided that they could go shopping on another day, to give Grandma a chance to rest a little more. However, as the evening came, Grandma's headache got worse and she decided that she needed to see a doctor. When he examined her, the physician did not immediately know what was causing her symptoms, but prescribed pain relievers and suggested that she call him if the symptoms continued.

The symptoms did indeed continue. The fever rose higher and the pain from her headache got worse. Grandma was admitted to the hospital, where she died of fatal encephalitis (an inflammation of the brain) just a couple of days later.

During the grandmother's last day at the hospital, the physicians met with her family to try to determine what had caused the sudden encephalitis. The family described the grandmother's last weekend as a perfectly normal one in which she had been full of energy and in high spirits. They explained that the worst thing that had happened to her was that she was bitten by a mosquito. A visiting doctor from Israel was at the hospital and pointed out that a mosquito bite a few days before an elderly women dies of encephalitis may be more than a passing coincidence. The physician explained that mosquitoes can sometimes carry a virus that causes encephalitis, and that birds, which can also be infected with the virus, are often a good indication of whether the virus is present in a specific area. The mother immediately remembered finding the dead blue jay in their yard on the same day that Grandma was bitten by the mosquito.

The hospital staff promptly performed specific tests to figure out whether this virus the Israeli doctor had mentioned, known as West Nile virus, was in the grandmother's body. The test indicated that the virus was, in fact, present. For the first time, West Nile virus had been detected in the United States. However, this *virus was not simply a normal strain (type) of West Nile virus. The strain that was now in the United States was nearly identical to a particularly deadly strain that had appeared in Israel just the year before. The Israeli physician explained that the West Nile virus was transmitted through mosquito bites, and that the mosquito bite on the grandmother's arm was very likely the source of the virus that had caused her death.*

Generally, most people infected with West Nile virus display no signs and have no symptoms. Approximately 20 percent of those infected develop a mild infection known as West Nile fever. Signs and symptoms of the fever include: nausea, vomiting, diarrhea, headache, backache, muscle aches, a skin rash, swollen lymph nodes, and a loss of appetite. The symptoms last three to six days and the patient recovers spontaneously and completely.

Less than 1 percent of those infected actually develop the grave form of the disease. This is a serious neurological infection that may include inflammation of the brain alone (**encephalitis**), or of the brain and the connective tissue membranes that surround and protect it (**meningoencephalitis**). Sometimes, only the membranes are affected and become inflamed (**meningitis**). Rarely, the spinal cord may become inflamed (**West Nile poliomyelitis**) causing a sudden weakness in the arms, legs, and breathing muscles. This form of the disease is accompanied by a high fever, a severe headache with a stiff neck, partial paralysis, lack of coordination, disorientation and confusion, and possible convulsions and coma. In patients who recover, encephalitis or meningitis may last for weeks and some neurological effects, such as muscle weakness, may be permanent.

Although the specific example of the attack of West Nile virus told above is fictitious, the panic that struck the people of the United States in the summer of 1999 with the first appearance of this deadly new strain of the West Nile virus was very real. Several factors made the panic even worse than it might have been if another disease had been the culprit. Currently, there are no medications that people can take to make the virus go away. Most often, hospitals can only provide treatment to relieve the pain associated with the symptoms of encephalitis. There simply is no cure for West Nile virus infection—at least not yet. Furthermore, the European strains of the virus have generally not been as harmful, which made the fact that the U.S. strain was deadly even scarier. Because the virus was not previously lethal, vaccine development had not been a priority for the pharmaceutical industry. Much effort has been put into finding a way to treat the people who do fall ill. Vaccine development became a priority and has met with some success (see chapter 7).

The West Nile virus that was introduced and isolated in New York in 1999 has rapidly spread to every corner of the United States and has reached as far as South America and Canada. The quick spread of West Nile virus to the vast geographies in which it is now present is primarily due to its natural transmission cycle. The virus exists among infected birds and is transmitted from one bird to another (called **hosts**) by biting mosquitoes. Thus, a single infected bird in a flock of migrating birds is able to spread West Nile virus across an entire continent in a single season. As mosquitoes feed on the blood of the infected bird in each state or country through which the birds fly, the virus is introduced into that region. Once there, the transmission cycle continues until a large proportion of the mosquitoes in the state carry the virus.

So, although mosquitoes have always been unwelcome guests at our summer pool parties and cookouts, they have rarely been more than a nuisance in the United States—that is, until the summer of 1999. Now mosquitoes also represent the threat of a virus that can be spread to our friends and family by a simple mosquito bite. The bite of a mosquito that carries the West Nile virus can generate a disease that causes severe headaches, fevers, fatigue, coma, or even death to the infected individual. This virus, which is relatively new to the United States, has struck fear in the minds of the American people.

2

A Foreign Virus Emerges in the United States

Although many diseases have been described since ancient times, the **pathogens** (germs) that cause these diseases have only recently been appreciated or even superficially understood. One example is an illness once described as brain fever, now more frequently referred to as encephalitis. In the early part of the 20th century, scientists discovered two viruses that infect the spinal cord and brain. These were the poliovirus (discovered by Karl Landsteiner in 1909) and the rabies virus (discovered by Joseph Lennox Pawan in 1931). By the 1940s, it became apparent that some neurological (brain-related) diseases of viral origin were different from the diseases caused by rabies and polioviruses. Also, the symptoms and **pathogenesis** (how the disease develops) of the infections were distinct. This suggested that more pathogens than just rabies and poliovirus were capable of causing the general symptom of encephalitis in humans.

In 1901, scientists had discovered that mosquitoes and ticks could transmit encephalitis. This finding further advanced the understanding of how viral encephalitis originated. Collectively, these newly discovered viruses spread by mosquitoes became known as arthropod-borne viruses, or **arboviruses**. (Mosquitoes, ticks, and many other biting insects are part of a group called **arthropods**.) These encephalitic arboviruses were further classified into four groups—A, B, C, and D—that were based on the symptoms of the disease and the region in which they were first discovered. The Group B arboviruses were eventually placed into a family, *Flaviviridae*, which was named after the disease yellow fever that is caused

THE PHYLUM ARTHROPODA

If there was ever a group of creatures that deserved to be the star of a movie, it is the phylum Arthropoda (which literally means "jointed feet"). In fact, many of the members of the phylum have been the focus of Hollywood. The phylum—which is a major division of the animal kingdom and includes insects, crustaceans, spiders, scorpions, barnacles, and centipedes—is very diverse (Figure 2.1). All of its members share certain common characteristics. First, the body is strongly segmented. The body segments of arthropods are loosely filled with tissue, sinuses (empty cavities), and blood. Additionally, members of the phylum may breathe through their body surface. The body surface of all of the members consists of an exoskeleton made of chitin (pronounced *kuy-tin*), a hard substance that can be created as a thin and flexible material or a thick rigid shell. The thick rigid shell is what most arthropods have as their exoskeleton. Once the animal outgrows its shell, the skeleton is shed off by a process called molting.

Despite these physical similarities among members, the phylum is extremely diverse. The sum of the species in all other phyla (plural of *phylum*) added together still does not surpass the number of species in the phylum Arthropoda. Some of the members of the phylum help sustain the world's ecological balance. However, many of the members are among the world's greatest pests. The most devastating plagues and famines that the world has known have been caused by arthropods, some of which are recurring threats. For example, grasshoppers often overbreed to proportions vast enough to destroy entire regions of crops. Additionally, the locusts of Africa routinely disrupt life for the people of the continent by destroying crops and crippling the economy.

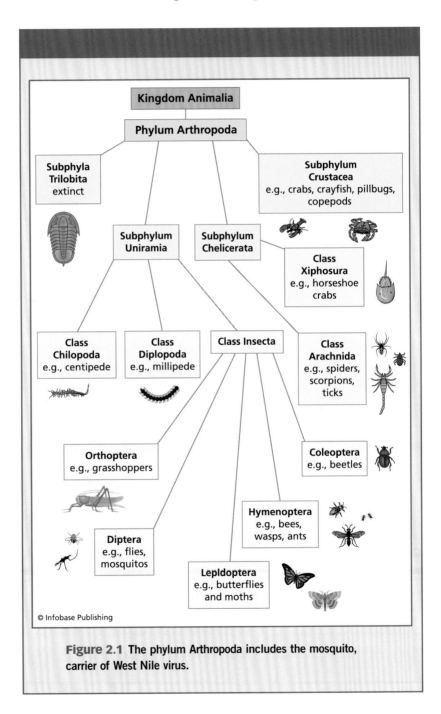

Figure 2.1 The phylum Arthropoda includes the mosquito, carrier of West Nile virus.

by one species in the family (the Latin term *flavus* means "yellow"). Today there are more than 70 identified viruses in the Flaviviridae family, one of which is West Nile virus.

DISCOVERY OF THE FLAVIVIRUS

The first **flavivirus** ever isolated is actually the virus family's namesake. In the early 1900s, an American army surgeon

Figure 2.2 Walter Reed, a U.S. Army surgeon and pioneer in human virus research, discovered that yellow fever was a virus and that it was transmitted by mosquitoes. (National Library of Medicine)

named Walter Reed (Figure 2.2) became a pioneer in human virus research by demonstrating through his experiments two groundbreaking concepts regarding the disease known as yellow fever. His first discovery, in 1901, demonstrated that mosquitoes transmitted yellow fever. A year later, Reed made an even more revolutionary discovery by showing that yellow fever could be transferred to another specimen through the filtered **serum** of an infected individual. This discovery suggested that the pathogen that caused yellow fever was not a bacterium, since bacteria particles are fairly large for **microorganisms**, and would have been removed from the serum during filtration. Instead, the experiment implied that the pathogen was much smaller, and more likely, a virus. Several years later, the cause of yellow fever was isolated and named yellow fever virus after the disease that the virus caused. The yellow fever virus was isolated in 1927, and became the first member of the Flaviviridae family to be isolated. In 1932, yellow fever virus was grown in a broth of cells and a special nutrient solution. This allowed vast quantities of the virus to be isolated for the first time, and allowed vaccines to be developed just a few years later.

DENGUE FEVER

The first documented epidemic caused by a member of the Flaviviridae family was dengue fever. The first report of a case of the disease may have been recorded in China during the Chin dynasty (A.D. 265–420). As early as the 1780s, epidemics occurred in North America, Africa, and Asia. In 1789, the famous American physician, Benjamin Rush (Figure 2.3), wrote the first case report on dengue fever. This disease is associated with an acute fever, a severe, long-lasting headache, severe muscle and joint pains (giving the disease the name **"breakbone fever"**), and rashes. Although neurological symptoms are not usually associated with the disease, several cases of **dengue encephalitis** have been reported.[1] The virus is spread by the *Aedes aegypti* mosquito rather than by the vari-

Figure 2.3 Benjamin Rush, the famous Amercian physician who wrote the first definitive case report on dengue fever. (National Library of Medicine)

ous species of the *Culex* mosquito that spread West Nile virus. Currently, the virus infects hundreds of thousands of people in the tropical Americas and countries of the Asia Pacific.

AUSTRALIAN X DISEASE

Other members of the Flaviviridae family were soon discovered as well. An early documented outbreak of encephalitis caused by a flavivirus occurred in Australia during the summer of 1917. At first it was incorrectly diagnosed as poliomyelitis, because patients showed the common symptom of inflamed nerve tissue. The outbreak affected 134 people, half of them under the age of five. Alarmingly, approximately 70 percent of the affected people died. Although efforts were made to collect and accurately identify the agent that caused the disease, microbiology was in a primitive state in its development at the time. The collected specimens were not successfully amplified or preserved, which left researchers unable to identify the pathogen. Eventually, all specimens of the pathogen were lost and future outbreaks were sporadic and less severe, making it even harder to collect additional samples. The illness became known as Australian X disease, and its cause was not determined until another severe outbreak occurred in 1951 around the Murray Valley region of Australia. More than 30 years after the first outbreak of Australian X disease, the virus responsible was finally isolated and grown from a specimen taken from a patient who had died of the disease in the same region of Australia. Additional specimens were also isolated from mosquitoes. The virus was named Murray Valley encephalitis virus, after the region where the virus was isolated. Similarities in the diseases made it likely that the pathogen that had caused Australian X disease in 1917 was the same as that identified in 1951.

ST. LOUIS ENCEPHALITIS

The next earliest reported cases of encephalitis outbreaks occurred in the United States. The first outbreak happened in Illinois during the summer mosquito breeding season of 1932, and another occurred in St. Louis, Missouri, during the summer of the following year. The virus responsible for these outbreaks was isolated and named St. Louis encephalitis virus after the region where the virus was identified. Eventually, the St. Louis encephalitis virus was found to be transmitted by mosquitoes and to infect rodents and humans, and was classified in the Flaviviridae family.

WEST NILE VIRUS

In December 1937, the virus that is now known as West Nile virus was isolated from an elderly woman with a mild fever who lived in the West Nile Province of Uganda in Africa. Surprisingly, this particular virus specimen was not associated with an outbreak of encephalitis. Initially, at least, West Nile virus was not associated with any illness. However, by 1951, the year of the first recorded West Nile virus outbreak associated with a disease, the virus had spread throughout Africa and the Middle East. The disease caused by West Nile virus infection, known then as West Nile fever, was actually very mild in 1951. Symptoms included a flu-like illness, consisting of a fever, headache, and general feeling of tiredness. During this outbreak, viral specimens were isolated in Egypt from children, birds, mosquitoes, and the brain of a horse with encephalitis. The outbreaks in Israel during 1951, 1953, and 1957 represent the first recorded epidemics caused by West Nile virus. Subsequently, epidemics have also occurred in France (1962) and in Romania (1966). One of the largest recorded epidemics occurred in South Africa in 1974, where 3,000 people were diagnosed with the disease.

The largest outbreak in history occurred during 2003 when more than 10,000 people in North America developed symptoms after being infected with West Nile virus.[2] The second largest outbreak in history took place between June 10 and December 31, 2002 when 4,156 cases of West Nile virus illness were diagnosed over 39 states and the District of Columbia.[3] The incidence of outbreaks has decreased drastically since 2003 (see Figure 2.4).

AN OUTBREAK OF ENCEPHALITIS
IN NEW YORK CITY

August 23, 1999, was a warm, cloudy day in New York City. So far it had been pretty much a routine day for a physician in northern Queens. The physician treated patients with a variety of illnesses as he did every day in the hospital. Two

TIMELINE OF MAJOR FLAVIVIRIDAE OUTBREAKS

1780   Dengue fever is found in Asia, Africa, and North America

1901   Yellow fever virus transmission by mosquitoes discovered

1917   Australian X outbreak

1927   Yellow fever virus isolated

1932   Yellow fever virus vaccines developed and used in humans; St. Louis encephalitis virus outbreak in Illinois

1933   St. Louis encephalitis virus outbreak in Missouri

1934   Tick-borne encephalitis virus outbreak in the Soviet Union

1945   Tick-borne encephalitis virus outbreak in central Europe

1951   Australian X outbreak; West Nile virus outbreak in Israel

1953   West Nile virus outbreak in France and Israel

1957   West Nile virus outbreak in Israel

1966   West Nile virus outbreak in Romania

1974   West Nile virus outbreak in South Africa

1996   West Nile virus outbreak in Romania

1998   West Nile virus outbreak in Italy and Israel

1999   West Nile virus outbreak in northeastern United States

2000   West Nile virus outbreak in the United States

2001   West Nile virus outbreak in Canada

2002   West Nile virus outbreak in the Caribbean and the United States

2003   West Nile virus outbreak in the United States

2005   Japanese encephalitis virus outbreak in India and Nepal

2006   West Nile virus outbreak in the United States; St. Louis encephalitis outbreak in Brazil

2007   West Nile virus outbreak in the United States and Canada

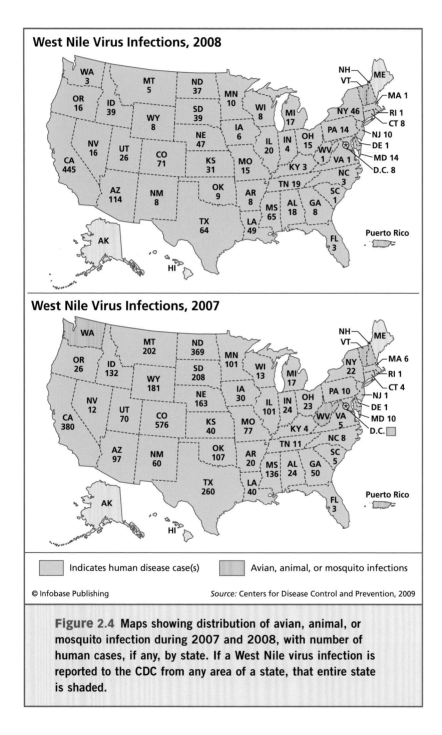

Figure 2.4 Maps showing distribution of avian, animal, or mosquito infection during 2007 and 2008, with number of human cases, if any, by state. If a West Nile virus infection is reported to the CDC from any area of a state, that entire state is shaded.

patients who came into the hospital were complaining of a headache and fever and both were admitted for evaluation. The cases were diagnosed as encephalitis and reported to the New York City Department of Health. Encephalitis is inflammation of the brain and can often be a serious and even fatal disease. Mild cases of encephalitis may only have symptoms of headache, loss of appetite, or a general uncomfortable feeling. However, in more severe cases, a person may suffer from a high fever, severe headache, nausea and vomiting, stiff neck, seizures, difficulty controlling voluntary movements, and even coma or death. Most cases of diagnosed encephalitis are caused by viral infections. Therefore, the potential seriousness of the disease requires that each case of encephalitis a physician finds be reported to the local department of health. At the time that the physician in northern Queens made his report of encephalitis, he had no idea that this routine call would come to represent the discovery of a deadly virus that had entered the United States for the first time in history.

Within days, six more patients were identified with similar symptoms of encephalitis. Five of these patients had profound muscle weakness and required mechanical assistance to keep their lungs breathing. All of these patients lived within a two-square-mile area in northern Queens, New York. This was an unusually high percentage of patients with similar severe symptoms and it meant that the disease-causing agent might be more **virulent** (able to infect the body) than the more common causes of encephalitis known to exist in the United States. These people had not been in contact with each other, either, which indicated that the disease was not an isolated event and that the mode of transmission was likely one that was common to the environment—like mosquitoes. The isolated geography of the cases also meant that there was hope that fast action by health officials might help keep the agent that was causing the disease contained within this relatively small area.

IDENTIFICATION OF WEST NILE VIRUS
IN THE UNITED STATES

During a period of weeks just before the outbreaks of human encephalitis, New York City health officials noticed an unusual increase in dead birds around the city. Although the sheer number of dead birds was sufficiently alarming for officials to record the event, the local officials did not take immediate action to determine the cause of these deaths. Most of the dead birds were crows, and there was no evidence that the disease that killed these birds could be transmitted to humans. However, in September 1999, just one month after the human cases of encephalitis were diagnosed, three captive birds—two flamingos and a pheasant—died while on display at the Bronx Zoo. An autopsy performed by zoo veterinarians found that the birds had encephalitis and severe **myocarditis**, an inflammation of the myocardium (the muscular tissue of the heart). Tissue samples from these birds were sent to the U.S. Department of Agriculture National Veterinary Services Laboratory (NVSL) in Ames, Iowa. The NVSL determined that the birds had been infected with West Nile virus and that this virus was likely the cause of their death.

All of the tissue and blood samples from the human cases in New York were retested for the presence of West Nile virus. The results of these tests clearly indicated that West Nile virus was causing the encephalitis cases in New York.

The identification of West Nile virus in tissue samples from the cases in the United States was both surprising and alarming. In a matter of weeks, a single report of two cases of encephalitis in New York led to the identification of a virus that had never been seen before in the Western Hemisphere. The summer of 1999 marked the first time that the West Nile virus was detected in the United States. In this single outbreak, 62 human encephalitis cases were reported; the disease resulted in the death of seven of these people. The implications of this new viral threat to Americans have been far-reaching, both from a health and an economic perspective.

HOW DID WEST NILE VIRUS ENTER
THE UNITED STATES?

Several theories exist for the introduction of West Nile virus into the Western Hemisphere. All of these theories result from the ease of intercontinental travel that we take for granted in today's society. One unlikely possibility is that an infected person brought the West Nile virus into the United States after traveling into the country. If this infected person was an otherwise healthy adult, he or she may not even have known that he or she was infected with the virus, since most people remain **asymptomatic** (showing no symptoms) throughout the course of the infection. However, as we will discuss in Chapter 5, for West Nile virus to spread, the infected person would have to be bitten by a mosquito outside of the United States and then pass the virus to another mosquito once inside the United States. Only then could the virus be circulated in the local environment through normal transmission cycles between birds and mosquitoes. Although this scenario is conceivable, it is probably the least likely of the proposed ways the virus might have come to America. As we will see, transmission of West Nile virus from humans to mosquitoes, rather than vice versa, is extremely rare.

A more likely possibility is that the initial source of the virus was either an infected bird or a mosquito. Both species have long life spans; birds can live several decades and female mosquitoes (which are the ones that bite humans) generally live longer than three months. Therefore, introduction by either species is equally plausible, since either could have lived long enough to make a boat trip across the Atlantic Ocean. Accidental introduction of the virus by a stowaway mosquito in a boat or a plane would easily carry the virus to birds upon the mosquito's arrival in the United States. Many types of sea birds, looking for an easy meal (such as scraps) from the incoming boats, are found at every seaport (Figure 2.5.). These birds unwittingly provide easy meals for mosquitoes, which drink their blood. Just as easily, an infected bird could have

Figure 2.5 Birds that nest on cargo ships that travel internationally may bring new diseases to an area. (© Rafael Ramirez Lee/ Shutterstock images)

accidentally been brought to the United States in the same way. Some of the large ships that transport goods across the sea are often followed by or provide homes to opportunistic birds that stow away on the ships. These birds may be temporarily scared away from the boat when the ship docks and begins to unload. An infected bird would have had the potential to introduce West Nile virus to the United States by being bitten by a mosquito in a U.S. port, thus introducing the virus to the local ecology. However, birds generally survive for only a few days after they are infected with West Nile virus. Therefore, the possibility that a bird introduced the virus to the United States via a transatlantic boat journey is less likely than the possibility that a mosquito provided the first introduction.

Other means of accidental introduction through birds have also been proposed, but they are not as likely as the stowaway scenario. Importation of exotic birds has the potential to introduce many pathogens into the destination country. However, because of this health risk, the U.S. customs service, through the U.S. Department of Agriculture (USDA), has imposed tight restrictions on the importation of birds. These import regulations are primarily put in place to protect the lucrative American poultry industry from the potential introduction of foreign diseases. As part of the restrictions, veterinary checkups are required immediately before and after birds are imported into the country and imported birds must also remain for a minimum of 30 days in quarantine at a U.S. Department of Agriculture Animal Import Center. The 30-day quarantine is enough time to allow the bird to either overcome the infection of West Nile virus (or other disease) through its own immune system, or succumb to the disease and no longer pose a threat. Unfortunately, illegal importation of birds is not subject to the same rigors as the legal routes. In fact, the only real restriction in the illegal trade is a "don't get caught" mentality that would actually have no effect whatsoever on the West Nile virus. The illegal importation of birds represents a real threat of having caused the outbreak of West Nile virus in the United States. However, it would be impossible to tell at this point whether the virus was introduced by a smuggled bird.

3

Structure and Function of the West Nile Virus

Viruses are microscopic particles that contain genetic information surrounded by a protein shell. The protein shell protects the virus as it travels from cell to cell or from organism to organism. The shell also helps the virus deliver its genetic information into a susceptible cell. A virus can only survive by living inside the cells of another organism (called a host). For this reason, some scientists do not even consider viruses living things, since they cannot survive on their own. In the case of West Nile virus, individual virus particles, or **virions**, are introduced into the bloodstream of a host through the bite of an infected mosquito. Then, the virus travels through the bloodstream to find a suitable cell in the body in which it can replicate (make copies of itself). Successful replication creates many new virions that then return to the bloodstream and look for additional cells to enter and use to replicate. This amplification of a single virion into many virions is known as the virus **replication cycle.**

The replication cycle of West Nile virus can be described in six general stages (Figure 3.1):

1. Attachment of the virion to the target cell

2. Entry into the cell

3. Replication of the viral genome

4. Synthesis of new viral subunits

5. Assembly of the subunits to form new virions

6. Release of the new virions

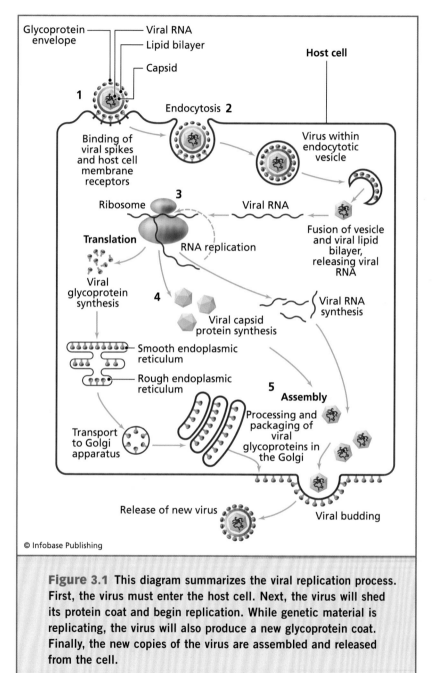

Glycoprotein envelope

Viral RNA

Lipid bilayer

Capsid

Host cell

1

Endocytosis **2**

Binding of viral spikes and host cell membrane receptors

Virus within endocytotic vesicle

3

Ribosome

Viral RNA

Translation

RNA replication

Fusion of vesicle and viral lipid bilayer, releasing viral RNA

Viral glycoprotein synthesis

4

Viral capsid protein synthesis

Viral RNA synthesis

Smooth endoplasmic reticulum

Rough endoplasmic reticulum

5

Assembly

Transport to Golgi apparatus

Processing and packaging of viral glycoproteins in the Golgi

Release of new virus

Viral budding

© Infobase Publishing

Figure 3.1 This diagram summarizes the viral replication process. First, the virus must enter the host cell. Next, the virus will shed its protein coat and begin replication. While genetic material is replicating, the virus will also produce a new glycoprotein coat. Finally, the new copies of the virus are assembled and released from the cell.

Each of these stages of the West Nile virus replication cycle will be described in this chapter. However, before discussing the specifics of the replication cycle, we first need to understand the general structure of the West Nile virus.

THE STRUCTURE OF THE WEST NILE VIRUS VIRION

A West Nile virus particle is spherical in shape and approximately 40 to 60 nanometers in diameter (Figure 3.2). To give you an idea of how tiny this is, if 2,000 West Nile virus particles were stacked on top of each other, the height of the stack would still be less than the thickness of a single dollar bill. Despite its small size, the ordered complexity of this microscopic virus particle is amazing. A view of the virion, looking crosswise through the middle of the particle, reveals three highly specific layers. Scientists have discovered that these layers are primarily made up of three different proteins and a lipid (fat) coat. The three proteins that make up the layers of the virion have been named the envelope protein, E; the membrane protein, M; and the capsid protein, C (this confers specificity on the virus). The outermost layer of the virion is formed by the E and M proteins (Figure 3.3). These two proteins are the first parts of the virion that interact with the host when the virus locates a host cell. The central core of the virion contains the

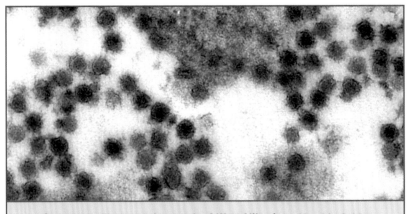

Figure 3.2 Electron micrograph of West Nile virus. (Cynthia Goldsmith/Centers for Disease Control and Prevention)

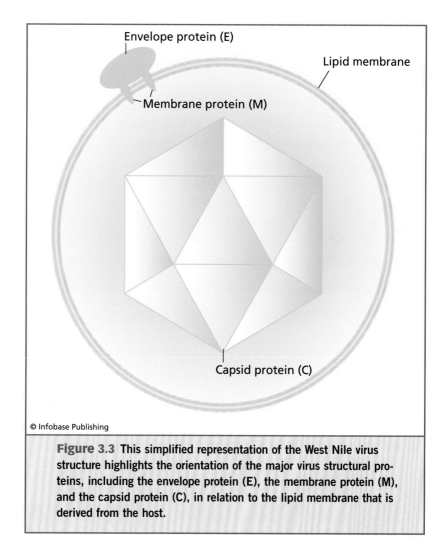

Figure 3.3 This simplified representation of the West Nile virus structure highlights the orientation of the major virus structural proteins, including the envelope protein (E), the membrane protein (M), and the capsid protein (C), in relation to the lipid membrane that is derived from the host.

ribonucleic acid (**RNA**) genetic material of West Nile virus and the C protein. Between the core and the outermost layer is a lipid coat that is actually made from the host cell as the viral proteins assemble to form the virion. These three proteins that form the ordered structure of the virion are collectively referred to as the "structural proteins." However, additional proteins are also needed to allow the virus to multiply, or replicate. Seven nonstructural proteins exist in West Nile virus that function like enzymes (body proteins that help make biochemical reactions work), but are not arranged in the virion in a way that supports the structure of the virion. These structural and nonstructural molecules direct and facilitate the six stages of the West Nile virus replication cycle.

THE WEST NILE VIRUS REPLICATION CYCLE
Attachment and Entry Into the Target Cell

The first stage of the West Nile virus replication cycle is attachment. This stage targets the cell that the virus will invade and then use to replicate itself. Since most cells in the body have highly specialized functions, they also have different compositions that

HOW NOT TO TRAP A VIRUS

Bacteria have been known to mankind for quite some time. They may be visualized using a standard compound microscope such as those found in lab classrooms all over the world. Viruses, however, are a whole different story. Most viruses range in size from five to 300 nanometers (a billionth of a meter), whereas bacteria typically range in size from one to five micrometers (a millionth of a meter), thus making them approximately one thousand times larger than viruses.

Bacterial size enabled the French microbiologist Charles Chamberland to create a filter in 1884 with pores smaller than bacteria. When he passed a solution containing bacteria through the filter, he was able to trap the bacteria in the filter, rendering the solution free of bacteria. Today, this filter is known as a Chamberland filter, or a Chamberland-Pasteur filter.

In 1892, the Russian biologist Dmitri Ivanovski was working with what is now known as tobacco mosaic virus (TMV), a virus that infects tobacco leaves, and repeated the filtration experiments that Chamberland performed. He was able to show that whatever it was that was damaging the tobacco leaves was small enough to pass through the filter and was allow them to perform their specific function. For example, the cells of the brain process our thoughts and behaviors, the cells of the immune system travel around the body to identify and eliminate infections, and epithelial cells (which make up the membranes and skin) define the structure and boundaries of our organs. This diversity of cells has limited the ability of viruses to replicate in all types of cells with equal efficiency. Some cells cannot support virus replication at all. Therefore, if the virus loses its ability to target only the cells that can support its replication, the virus may doom its replication cycle before it has even created its first new virion.

therefore much smaller than bacteria. Not being able to visualize the virus, Ivanovski never actually identified the cause of the disease and stopped his research.

In 1899, the Dutch microbiologist Martinus Beijerinck repeated Ivanovski's experiments and concluded that the disease was caused by a new form of infectious agent. He even showed that the agent needed living cells to multiply. However, due to the virus' size, he could never visualize it.

Many researchers in several countries continued working with TMV and several other viruses over the years and made numerous discoveries that helped in the understanding of how viruses work. Finally, in 1931 the electron microscope was invented, thus allowing researchers to actually see viruses. TMV was visualized in 1935 by Wendell Stanley.

It is important to note that one virus, vaccinia (the virus that causes cowpox and was used by Jenner to vaccinate against smallpox), was actually visualized in 1887 by Scottish pathologist John Buist using a standard compound microscope and stain. The virus is approximately 360 nanometers in size and is barely visible using a standard microscope.

ICOSAHEDRAL SYMMETRY

Although viruses have diverse characteristics in genetic makeup, form, and host range, they have some commonalities in their structure. Four scientists have been largely credited with discovering the mechanisms of virus assembly. The first two scientists, James Watson and Francis Crick, are more famous for their work in discovering the structure of deoxyribonucleic acid (DNA). However, they also made important theoretical contributions toward understanding virus structure. One contribution was the concept that the virus genome was probably too small to code for more than a few proteins. This meant that the virus must use the same type of molecule many times to assemble the complex shell. This idea was called the theory of identical subunits. This theory led to the development of a second theory, which stated that symmetry must be imposed in order to efficiently assemble the same protein into a shell. Such a complex process that was limited in the types of building blocks available could not possibly be assembled randomly in an efficient manner. The imposed symmetry provided efficiency to virus assembly that could be determined mathematically. These theories have been proven by experimentation, and it is known that viruses use icosahedral (having the shape of a

The E protein of West Nile virus has the function of finding a cell that can support the virus's replication cycle by probing the surface of all the cells of the body, looking for specific characteristics. These so-called markers usually have functions that are vital to the cell's survival, but they can also serve as potential "receptors" for the virus. Once the E protein identifies the specific receptor it wants, which indicates that the cell can support replication of the virus, the virion

20-sided figure) symmetry to form their capsid from identi-cal subunits.

Another team of scientists, Don Caspar and Aaron Klug, later calculated that an icosahedral virus was made of 20 equal-sized faces. The scientist described a brilliant model in which the equally sized faces were made of the same protein used over and over to create triangles that could fit together to form the icosahedron. This concept allowed sci-entists to explain how relatively small proteins could com-bine to form larger faces and, therefore, larger-sized viruses. However, these identical subunits would have to exist in slightly different local environments. Some of the proteins would reside at an axis with five-fold symmetry and others at an axis with six-fold symmetry. These different environ-ments were defined to be occupied by the same protein, which would have to adopt slightly different shapes as dictated by the local symmetry. These subtle differences in shape were described by Caspar and Klug as quasi-equivalence. During a span of one decade, from 1955 to 1965, these four scientists described general concepts that are still taught today as the fundamentals of virus structure and self-assembling molecules.

attaches to the receptor and is able to get inside the cell. The receptor of West Nile virus has not been identified yet, and scientists believe the virus may use more than one kind of receptor for entry.

Replication of the Genome

For all virus families, the virus possesses the genetic code that defines the proteins that make up the virion and dictates how the

WHAT THE INFLUENZA VIRUS TAUGHT SCIENTISTS ABOUT WEST NILE VIRUS

Much of our knowledge about virus entry is the result of experiments performed with the hemagglutinin (a kind of protein) molecule of the influenza virus (Figure 3.4). The hemagglutinin molecule was named for its general property of causing clumping, or agglutination, of red blood cells. The influenza virus hemagglutinin is packed on the outside of influenza virions and appears as spikes on the particles. The molecule is the complementary protein of the West Nile virus E protein. These molecules reach out and bind sugar molecules on the target cell that the virus is going to infect. In particular, the virus binds to sialic acid molecules that are abundant on the surface of most cells. The portion of the molecule that binds to the sialic acid is at the very top of the hemagglutinin molecule. After binding, the influenza virus is internalized by the cell, in a way similar to that described for West Nile virus. The acidic nature of the compartments that take in the virus triggers a change in the hemagglutinin molecule that causes a portion of the protein, known as the fusion peptide, to insert into the target cell's membrane. The conformational change that the proteins undergo when exposed to acidic environments was an extraordinary discovery. Two scientists were responsible for making this discovery: Don Wiley of Harvard University and Sir John Skehel of the National Institute for Medical Research in London, England. Wiley and Skehel's discovery

virions must replicate. The genome (all of an organism's genetic material) of the West Nile virus is contained on a single strand of approximately 11,000 nucleotides, known as RNA. After the West Nile virus enters the cell, its RNA genome immediately begins to create new virus proteins.

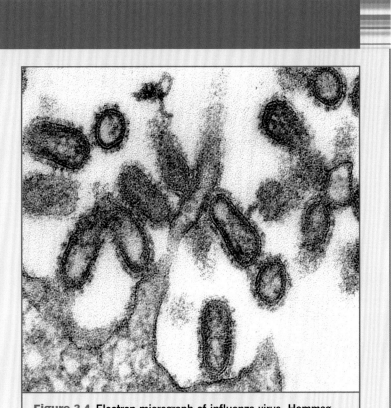

Figure 3.4 Electron micrograph of influenza virus. Hemmagglutinin appears as spikes on the virus particles. (C.S. Goldsmith; T. Tumpey/Centers for Disease Control and Prevention)

showed how viral proteins could help the virus fuse with the host cell's membrane and how proteins could undergo dramatic changes in shape.

The first proteins that are created play a role in various aspects of the replication cycle. At least one of the functions of these proteins is to bind to membranes within the host cell and begin copying the RNA genome. This process of amplification of the genome occurs in a cascade of events. Each new copy of the genome can serve as a model to create 10 more copies of the virus, while these 10 copies can each serve as a model to make 10 more copies. The cycle continues until the limits of the host cell, which provides the building materials for the RNA, are reached.

Creation (Synthesis) of New Viral Proteins

Once West Nile virus has gained entry into a host cell and unpacked its RNA genome, the process of making viral proteins begins at the same time as the replication process of the RNA genome described in the previous section. These cycles are intertwined. They begin with the proteins working to create more RNA, while the RNA, in turn, serves as a template to help produce more protein.

The RNA contains the genetic information needed to produce more protein. At first, the RNA directs the generation of one large protein, known as a polyprotein. The polyprotein actually contains all of the different proteins that make up any given virion. Most of the viral proteins are not active, or functional, when they are in the form of the polyprotein. They only become functional after they have been cut apart by an enzyme known as a protease. There are two subgroups of proteins that make up the West Nile virus virion: structural proteins and nonstructural proteins. The structural proteins play a part in the processes of assembly around the RNA genome, while the nonstructural proteins function in the replication of the RNA of the virus.

Structural Proteins

As the structural proteins are synthesized, they wrap around the cell's membrane to create the lipid coat of the virus. As a result, many of the structural proteins are found on both the inside and the outside of the virion. **Biosynthesis** (the production of a new chemical compound; in this case, new virions) begins in the **cytoplasm** of the cell with the capsid protein, or C protein. As biosynthesis continues, a specific part of the C protein sticks out through the cell membrane and the process continues translating into regions of the RNA that code for the matrix protein, or M protein. Most of the M protein is created on the side of the membrane opposite to the C protein. The M protein passes through the lipid layer twice before the region that will become the E protein is made.

These various structural proteins play the primary roles in the assembly, release, and entry stages of the virus's replication cycle.

Nonstructural Proteins

The nonstructural proteins get their name from their apparent lack of contribution to the overall structure of the virion. These proteins cannot be easily seen in images (called micrographs, taken with an electron microscope) of the West Nile virus, since they are spread throughout the central core of the virus. The nonstructural proteins are also the most difficult viral proteins to which we can conclusively assign a role in the viral replication cycle. Some nonstructural proteins seem to have multiple roles in the replication cycle of a virus, while others seem curiously useless in the process of replication. Although this may seem puzzling, keep in mind that the virus requires roles for some proteins when it invades certain cell species, but not for others. For example, the environment of a mosquito cell may be very different from that of a human cell, yet the virus must be prepared to replicate itself in either of these environments. One thing that all nonstructural proteins have in common is their localization to the site of RNA replication, termed the "replicase," and their importance to the completion of the replication cycle.

The replicase is a specific area in the cytoplasm of the cell that the virus creates for the purpose of replicating its RNA and generating new proteins. The nonstructural proteins work to establish the replicase and also perform the enzymatic functions that make replication easier. However, the functions of the individual proteins are frequently difficult to determine, because of the multiple and sometimes overlapping roles that the proteins play in the replication cycle. Some of the nonstructural proteins set up the location of the replicase. Once the initial location is determined by the binding of these proteins to a membrane in the cytoplasm, other nonstructural proteins come to the membrane and help link the other nonstructural proteins to the replicase. Many of the nonstructural proteins that are later linked to the replicase serve direct roles in the processes of copying the viral RNA. One of the most challenging tasks of studying viruses is understanding how these nonstructural proteins function. The task is difficult because the West Nile virus has several different hosts and must be prepared to use each differently for replication.

Assembly of New Virions

An interesting aspect of flavivirus replication is that RNA replication and viral assembly have seemingly distinct sites. The nonstructural proteins direct the replication of the genome at the replicase, while the structural proteins assemble virions around a portion of replicated RNA at another spot. This process of assembling virions begins with the binding of patches on the surface of the C protein to the newly replicated viral RNA. Many C proteins continue to bind to the RNA and wrap around the RNA as they compress and fold the nucleic acids to form a highly ordered polyhedron—an object that has 20 sides, defined as an icosahedral shell. This icosahedral shell, which is made of viral RNA and proteins, is generally known as a nucleocapsid. The RNA component of the nucleocapsid will eventually become the genome of the newly assembled virus. The nucleocapsid is then recruited to a site within the cell's cytoplasm that is occupied by the M and E proteins. These proteins, along with the membrane, envelop the nucleocapsid and separate from the rest of the cellular membrane. The result is an isolated virion within the host's cell.

A fascinating general feature of virus assembly is that while the components of the virus must come together in order to assemble a virion, the same components must disassemble when the virion enters the next cell. The proteins of the virus shell have become highly evolved to achieve this complicated assembly/disassembly feat. Both processes require energy that comes from both the host and the viral proteins. The virus may manipulate host proteins to achieve the biochemical reactions needed to assist in the assembly reaction. Afterward, the viral proteins are encapsulated by the viral membrane, which helps maintain the high concentration of assembled proteins inside the lipid coat. Usually, during the release stage, or shortly after, viral proteases (enzymes that split proteins) often digest the assembled viral proteins that make the core less stable. After the E protein helps the virus fuse into the cytoplasm of the next target cell, the less-stable, digested core is better suited to disassemble and start the replication process again.

Release of New Virions

New West Nile virus virions are released from the infected cell through a pathway that the cell normally uses to secrete proteins into the organism's bloodstream. Thus, the virus takes advantage of the host cell's trafficking pathways to make its way out of the cells it has infected and used to replicate itself. With the release of virions from infected cells, the process of searching for a new cell to infect can begin.

4

A Virus Transmitted by Mosquitoes

Harris was a college student majoring in ornithology, the study of birds. His primary interest was in birds of the family Corvidae such as crows and ravens. From 2005 through early 2008, he spent a good deal of time observing the wild crows that populated his rural neighborhood.

Now that summer had arrived and college classes were over until the fall semester, Harris had an opportunity to spend even more time observing "his" crows and keeping notes on their relative population density.

As the summer wore on, Harris noticed something very interesting and disturbing at the same time. The number of crows in the area was steadily declining. Nothing about the climate should have been contributing to this as it was a comfortable, warm summer with good weather patterns. In addition to this, he noticed that during his walks in the forest, he came across more and more dead crows.

This was very disturbing to him, so he visited the local health department to report his discovery. The employees promised Harris that they would look into it and told him not to worry about it. Still, he was very disturbed by the situation and wanted some answers.

One day, while reading the local paper, Harris noticed an article that discussed the unusual rise in the local mosquito population. He never liked mosquitoes, so he was now even more disturbed about what was taking place in his once peaceful and enjoyable neighborhood.

A short time later, Harris read an article in the local newspaper that described a disease that had killed four of the town's elderly inhabitants.

Their case histories were all very similar. Each had been admit-
ted to the hospital complaining of severe headaches, a high fever,
disorientation, muscle tremors, and lack of coordination. Shortly
after admission each one fell into a coma and eventually died.
This certainly stimulated the interest of the health department
and an investigation was started.

It turned out that the four victims did not know each other
and had nothing in common, with one exception. There were
several areas with standing water close to each of their houses.
In addition, these bodies of water were rather filled with large
mosquito populations.

Clearly, what had happened here was transmission of West
Nile virus from the crows to the humans via the mosquitoes.
Although the crows were a natural reservoir for the virus, the
humans had become incidental hosts and succumbed to the dis-
ease just as the many dead crows had.

Since 1999, thousands of people in the United States have
been infected with West Nile virus after being bitten by a mosquito, which is the primary mode of transmission of the virus.
This mode of transmission has caused a deep panic in many
Americans, because mosquitoes do not discriminate against
the source of their blood meal. Nearly every person is worried
that a loved one or even him- or herself may be the next person to be bitten by a mosquito that carries the deadly virus.
Although precautions to avoid mosquito bites, such as insect
repellent sprays, are often effective, they can be extremely
inconvenient to use every time you leave the protection of
your home.

WEST NILE VIRUS TRANSMISSION CYCLE

Part of the ability of the West Nile virus to rapidly become an
epidemic, an outbreak of a contagious disease that spreads
quickly and widely, is due to its transmission cycle, or how
the pathogen is passed from host to host. For arboviruses,

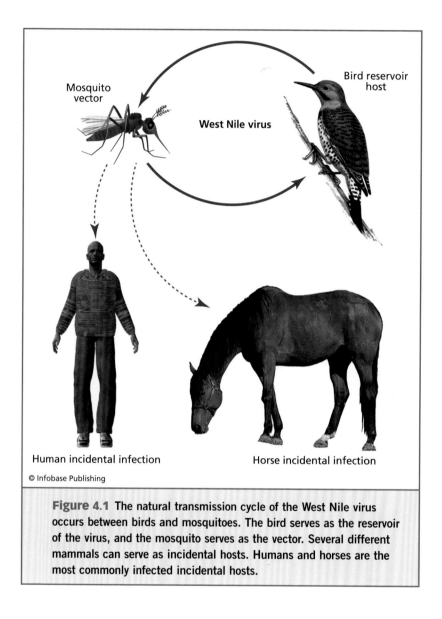

Mosquito
vector

West Nile virus

Bird reservoir
host

Human incidental infection

Horse incidental infection

© Infobase Publishing

Figure 4.1 The natural transmission cycle of the West Nile virus occurs between birds and mosquitoes. The bird serves as the reservoir of the virus, and the mosquito serves as the vector. Several different mammals can serve as incidental hosts. Humans and horses are the most commonly infected incidental hosts.

arthropods play the key role in spreading the virus. West Nile virus is mainly transmitted by mosquitoes, a member of the arthropod family.

There are two primary transmission routes for West Nile virus (Figure 4.1). The route indicated by curved red arrows depicts the spread of the virus between mosquitoes and birds. This portion of the transmission cycle is bidirectional, meaning that the virus can be transmitted either from mosquito to bird or from bird to mosquito. Transmission generally occurs when the mosquito lands on the bird and proceeds to bite it in order to suck the blood. Thus, the mosquito is the organism that carries West Nile virus between different organisms and therefore represents the **vector** of the pathogen. The vector is the organism that carries the virus from one animal to another. The mosquito does this by feeding frequently on the blood of birds during the mosquito-breeding season (usually during the late summer months). When this normal blood-meal feeding occurs, a mosquito that is infected with West Nile virus transmits the virus to the bird. The virus replicates in the bird and new virus builds up in the bird's bloodstream. When another mosquito later bites the infected bird, the virus passes to the mosquito with the blood meal. This transmission cycle between birds and mosquitoes continues throughout the mosquito-breeding season, and can cause the virus to spread throughout an entire state or even a larger geographical region.

The dashed arrows on the transmission cycle (refer again to Figure 4.1) point toward a cycle that is referred to as the dead-end route of the cycle. The organism that is not capable of transmitting the virus to another organism or back to the mosquito is called an **incidental host**, or a dead-end host. For West Nile virus, humans and horses (also called equines) are the most common incidental hosts. Both the human and equine hosts commonly become infected with West Nile virus after being bitten by an infected mosquito. However, the virus does not accumulate in the blood of the incidental host to a level that allows other mosquitoes to acquire the virus during subsequent blood-meal feedings. Thus, incidental hosts become infected with the pathogen and may show symptoms of disease, but generally, the incidental host cannot pass on the virus to other hosts.

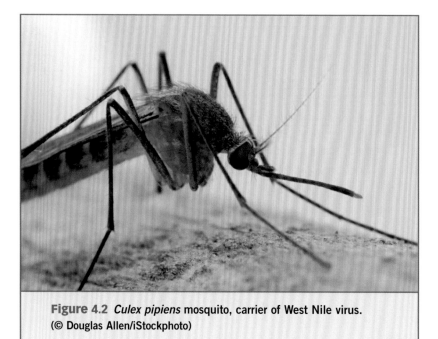

Figure 4.2 *Culex pipiens* mosquito, carrier of West Nile virus. (© Douglas Allen/iStockphoto)

When humans and horses become incidental hosts they do so because mosquitoes have become bridge vectors. What this means is that the mosquitoes in question don't normally feed on the humans or the horses, but usually take their blood meals from various species of birds. For whatever reason, these mosquitoes deviated from their normal feeding pattern and took a blood meal from the human or the horse and transmitted the West Nile virus to the incidental or dead-end host. In a recent study, *Culex pipiens* (Figure 4.2) mosquitoes collected in suburban Chicago in 2005 were studied to determine which species they had fed on.[1]

In order to do this the mosquitoes were ground up and polymerase chain reaction (PCR) and DNA sequencing techniques were used to analyze the DNA from the blood meals the mosquitoes had taken. It was determined that the mosquitoes had fed on 18 species of birds, most commonly the house spar-

HOW TO IDENTIFY WHAT MOSQUITOES HAVE BEEN EATING

Mosquitoes are very small insects that aren't easily seen in the environment. Many mosquitoes also have limited feeding times, which makes it very difficult for scientists to observe what they eat. So how do scientists know what a mosquito feeds on?

The first task in figuring out what a mosquito had for dinner is to catch the mosquito. Mosquitoes can be caught in several ways. One method involves using a box that catches resting mosquitoes in their habitat. Another way to catch mosquitoes is by using a cloud of carbon dioxide, which makes the mosquitoes pass out, allowing collectors to carefully pick up the motionless bodies.

Once gathered, the mosquitoes are categorized by species and then put into a blender to homogenize the tissue (break it down into very small particles of about equal size). The homogenized mosquitoes are then put through a test called an **ELISA** assay. This test is designed to detect a broad range of mammalian, avian, reptile, and amphibian **antigens** (substances that stimulate the body to start an immune response). A positive test for any of these antigens indicates what type of animal the mosquito has been feeding on. This analysis can be further clarified through polymerase chain reaction (PCR) assays, tests that detect the species-specific DNA that is contained within the blood being studied. Analysis by PCR can identify exactly which species a mosquito chose for its last meal. However, this type of assay is usually difficult to perform, because the blood samples can be easily contaminated and the technique is extremely sensitive. Therefore, the assay involves some predictions and planning before it is used. For example, if the ELISA assay indicates that the mosquito has been feeding on birds, then the PCR analysis will be designed to tell apart the different bird species living in the immediate area. These types of analysis have been used regularly to identify the meals of mosquitoes.

row, mourning dove, and American robin. However, it was also shown that four mammalian species had been fed upon by the mosquitoes. The majority were humans and raccoons. This last fact would incriminate *Culex pipiens* as a bridge vector for West Nile virus.

Exceptions to this general rule have been observed in rare cases. One example cites a hawk that died in the middle of winter due to an infection of West Nile virus. This reported infection was surprising for two reasons. First, mosquitoes are not active during winter, so the infection was not likely to be a new one. Second, birds that die from West Nile virus normally do so within one to seven days after becoming infected. Therefore, it was proposed that this hawk acquired the virus from an unknown vector or an unknown host reservoir that could live through the winter season—unlike mosquitoes. (A **reservoir** is an organism that directly or indirectly transmits a pathogen while being virtually immune to its effects.) A likely candidate for the unknown reservoir may have been an infected rodent that was eaten by the hawk. For example, a mouse might have maintained a low level of the West Nile virus circulating in its bloodstream and then been unlucky enough to be spotted by the hawk. The death of a hawk due to West Nile virus during a season when mosquitoes do not feed provided compelling evidence that undefined mechanisms of transmission *do* exist, possibly through what is normally considered an incidental host. However, it should be noted that this incident represents an exception to the usual rule of West Nile virus transmission, and it is well understood that birds are the main reservoir of West Nile virus during the mosquito-breeding season.

VIREMIA AND THE HOST RESERVOIR

The difference between an incidental host and a host reservoir for West Nile virus depends on one thing: the concentration of the virus in the bloodstream of the host. For West Nile virus, the likelihood that a bird or human being will be able to spread the virus depends on the probability that the mosquito ingested a West Nile virus particle when it fed on the blood of that organism. Whether the mosquito ate some of the virus during feeding directly depends on how much of the virus was present in the bloodstream of the organism on which the mosquito fed. If a host's bloodstream is packed full with virions, then each time a mosquito feeds on the host, the mosquito will almost certainly ingest a virion. However, if the host has low concentrations of virions in its bloodstream, then many mosquitoes may feed on the host and never ingest a single virion. The specific term that refers to the concentration of virions in the bloodstream of a host is **viremia**. When virions exist in high enough concentrations in the bloodstream to spread the illness, the host is said to have infectious viremia (Figure 4.3).

Birds are the most common organisms that transmit West Nile virus to mosquitoes and have been defined as the primary reservoir of West Nile virus. Birds are readily capable of sustaining infectious viremia of West Nile virus for one to four days after first being infected by the virus. During these days of infectious viremia, mosquitoes that feed on the infected bird acquire the virus along with the blood meal. However, after about four days, the infected bird's immune system either adapts to the pathogen by developing **antibodies** to the West Nile virus or clears it from its body, or the bird dies of the disease caused by the infection. If the bird's immune system adapts to West Nile virus, it acquires lifelong immunity to future infections by the virus. Surprisingly, most birds do not die from West Nile virus infections, but are more likely to develop immunity to the virus after becoming infected. Thus, a bird's ability to generate and maintain infectious viremia for a limited time and then develop immunity to the virus defines it as a host reservoir.

The fact that most birds do not die after becoming infected with West Nile virus may seem puzzling, since the popular media has portrayed a dead bird as an indication of

MALARIA

Malaria is another disease that is spread by mosquitoes and is often fatal. The disease is caused by a parasite that is transmitted from person to person by the female *Anopheles* mosquito. Humans are not a dead-end host for malaria, so the mosquito vector can become infected with the parasite if it chooses an infected human for a blood meal. Once introduced into the human, the parasite, known as *Plasmodium*, begins to grow in the liver cells. After the initial growth phase, parasites start to target the red blood cells of the host. Replication of the parasite inside the red blood cells destroys the cells as new parasites are released into the bloodstream, where the cycle can be continued. The blood stage parasite, known as a gametocyte, is ingested with the blood meal of the mosquito.

In the mosquito, the parasite follows a different life cycle that is not harmful to the mosquito. By 10 to 18 days after a mosquito has become infected with *Plasmodium*, the gametocytes enter a stage in which they are called sporozoites. They can be found in the mosquito's salivary glands. As with West Nile virus, when the mosquito bites a human host, it spits substances into the host's bloodstream to prevent blood clots from forming, and in this process, the *Plasmodium* is passed along as well.

The disease caused by the *Plasmodium* parasite, malaria, can vary in its degree of severity. Severe malaria causes abnormalities in the patient's blood and metabolism. Likewise, it may cause failure of the heart, liver, kidneys, and brain. Temperature and humidity are critical for the growth cycle of the parasite. As a result, malaria mainly occurs in tropical and subtropical regions of the world. The impact of malaria is heavy in the regions where the disease is spread. In fact, nearly one million people die worldwide each year from the disease.

the presence of West Nile virus in an area. In particular, the hooded crow (*Corvus corone*) has emerged as a symbol of West Nile virus activity in the United States. Although most birds do not die from West Nile virus, the strain that was introduced to the United States during the summer of 1999 seemed to be especially virulent, as is indicated by the more frequent appearance of dead birds, compared with earlier outbreaks of the virus that happened in Europe. Additionally, the crow is more

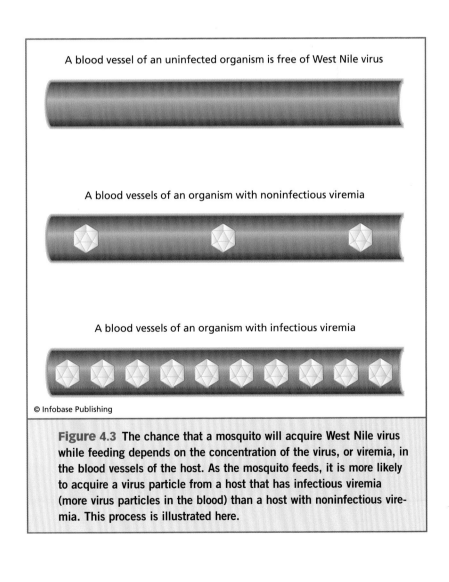

A blood vessel of an uninfected organism is free of West Nile virus

A blood vessels of an organism with noninfectious viremia

A blood vessels of an organism with infectious viremia

© Infobase Publishing

Figure 4.3 The chance that a mosquito will acquire West Nile virus while feeding depends on the concentration of the virus, or viremia, in the blood vessels of the host. As the mosquito feeds, it is more likely to acquire a virus particle from a host that has infectious viremia (more virus particles in the blood) than a host with noninfectious viremia. This process is illustrated here.

vulnerable to West Nile virus than other American birds. The crow's susceptibility could be a result of several factors. Mosquitoes may feed more frequently on crows than on other birds, a crow's immune system may be less efficient at eliminating the virus, or the crow may have certain genetic traits that give West Nile virus an advantage for rapidly replicating inside the bird's body cells. Though unfortunate for the crow, the fact that this bird species is quite susceptible to West Nile virus infections has provided medical professionals with a convenient way to tell that there has been an onset of virus activity in a particular region. The usefulness of monitoring West Nile virus activity through crows will be further explored in Chapter 7.

It is important to note that, although birds, particularly crows, seem to be the most important reservoirs for West Nile virus, tree squirrels are also an important reservoir. Research done in 2005 showed that tree squirrels are susceptible to West Nile virus-associated neurologic disease. In fact, their infection prevalence is comparable to that of dead birds.[2] The three species of tree squirrels that tested positive were the fox squirrel (*Sciurus niger*) (Figure 4.4), western gray squirrel (*Sciurus griseus*), and the eastern gray squirrel (*Sciurus carolinensis*). Some of the squirrels that were naturally infected with West Nile virus had levels of viremia (virus in the blood) sufficient enough to potentially infect mosquitoes. This would make these squirrels another reservoir for the disease in addition to birds.

Another interesting finding was that at least half of the tree squirrels infected were found to shed West Nile virus in their oral secretions. In fact, West Nile virus RNA was detected in fecal, oral, and urine samples of squirrels that were experimentally infected. This suggests that tree squirrels might be likely to transmit the virus via contact to cagemates or siblings, a mode of transmission also seen in birds.

OTHER ROUTES OF TRANSMISSION

It is important to point out that because most incidental hosts of West Nile virus do not generate infectious viremia

Figure 4.4 *Sciurus niger* or fox squirrel, known carrier of West Nile virus. (© Chas/shutterstock images)

does not mean that the virions are not replicating and are not infectious within such hosts. For instance, when humans are infected with West Nile virus by a mosquito bite, the virus replicates in the body, may cause disease in the person, and is usually cleared by the immune system. However, the viremia never reaches a high enough concentration so that another mosquito will ingest a virion when it feeds on the host. Thus, the new virions created in the human, and many other mammals, usually never leave the body of the host. Unfortunately, there are other routes of transmission for West Nile virus that are less easily identified than transmission through mosquito bites.

West Nile virus can potentially be spread through blood transfusions. However, questionnaires and screening of blood and blood donors are reasonably effective measures that prevent transmission via this route. In the state of South

Dakota, six cases of transmission via blood transfusion were reported in 2003 and one more in 2004. In 2006 a case of the disease was reported in the recipient of a kidney transplant from an infected donor.[3] In Arizona, a case of transfusion-associated West Nile virus occurred in 2004.[4] Since these cases were discovered, new tests have been designed to detect even very small amounts of the virus in donated blood, which should effectively prevent future transmissions of West Nile virus through blood transfusions.

Two other routes of transmission are also possible. A single case has been reported for transmission of West Nile virus from a mother to an infant through breast milk, and another individual case has been reported of transmission from a mother to her unborn infant across the placenta. However, these single cases represent a very small percentage of the total number of West Nile virus infections and are not common routes of transmission.

MOSQUITO VECTORS

Mosquitoes are the main source of transmission of West Nile virus infections for new organisms. Although West Nile has been identified in more than 46 different kinds of mosquitoes, the *Culex* species is thought to be primarily responsible for transmitting the virus. The causes that allow the *Culex* species to transmit the virus more efficiently than other species are not yet fully understood. The *Culex* mosquito is primarily **ornithophilic**, meaning that most of its blood meals come from birds. It is also known that a proportion of its blood meals comes from mammals. Thus, this species has the potential to spread the virus from its host reservoir, the bird, to incidental hosts, including humans. Another characteristic of this mosquito species is that the *Culex* prefers to live in an urban environment, and the female mosquitoes prefer to lay their eggs in man-made containers (like birdbaths) that collect nutrient-rich water. These characteristics make the *Culex* mosquito an ideal vector for the West Nile virus, since it has a diverse host feeding range and lives in an urban setting that helps it find many hosts on which to feed.

The West Nile virus initially exists in a transmission cycle primarily between birds and mosquitoes. As the transmission season progresses, the sheer number of mosquitoes that are infected with West Nile virus grows and directly causes the number of birds that have been bitten by infected mosquitoes to increase. This amplification in the numbers of both hosts and vectors consequently produces a higher incidence of dead-end host infections. Therefore, the virus is circulated in a cycle between nonhuman species until it has been sufficiently amplified, which makes the potential for human infections rise.

The cycle may not be as straightforward as this, however. There are still interesting questions concerning the dead-end host. Is an increase in dead-end host infections solely due to the increased ratio of mosquitoes that are infected with West Nile virus? If this were the case, we would have to assume that the *Culex* mosquito indiscriminately takes blood meals from both birds and mammals during the breeding season. Some scientists disagree with this assumption. An alternative explanation for increased human infection as the mosquito-breeding season progresses is that the initial transmission cycle exists only between bird species and the mosquito species. The transmission to dead-end hosts results only after a decrease in the availability of bird blood meals, due to birds that have either moved away from the region or died. The lack of bird hosts results in a shift to mammalian blood meals for the mosquitoes. The increase in human infections, then, is a result of ecological changes that make it more convenient for the mosquitoes to bite people rather than birds.

It is also worth noting that the *Culex* species of mosquito undergoes a type of hibernation during the winter season, similar to the hibernation of mammals. This survival of the mosquito over the course of the winter season provides a convenient mechanism to maintain the presence of the virus from year to year. Understanding all aspects of the transmission cycle of West Nile virus provides us with information that can be used to prevent additional spread of the virus and deaths caused by the disease.

5

How West Nile Virus Causes Disease

Once a mosquito that is carrying the West Nile virus lands on a person and starts to suck blood, the mosquito has started a chain of events that can lead to varying degrees of disease, from an infection that goes completely unnoticed to a fatal illness. Once West Nile virus enters an organism, it must locate a cell to enter that can support replication of the virus. The West Nile virus's ability to overwhelm the resources of the cell that it enters is the way the virus causes disease. But why is the disease more or less severe in different people and different organisms? The answer to this question relies on several factors, including the amount of virus that initially enters the body, the ability of the individual's immune system to create antibodies to West Nile virus, and which cells within the new host are infected. Interestingly, the mosquito that has the ability to put all of these events into motion, does so because it is unable to make an eggshell for its offspring, and because it has a special chemical that prevents human blood from clotting.

WHY DO MOSQUITOES BITE?

The transmission of West Nile virus begins with a mosquito's bite. In fact, it is not simply any mosquito, but only the female mosquito that bites other animals. Mosquitoes rely on nectar as their primary food source, just like bees and many other insects. However, during mating season, a female mosquito needs to lay eggs in a water source in order to hatch larvae, or baby mosquitoes. Finding a water source is the easy part of this cycle. The hard part is the need to produce a protective shell for the egg, similar to the shell of the chicken eggs you see at the grocery store, and this is what drives the mosquito to its vampire-like behavior. The female mosquito lacks the ability to produce the substances that make up the protective eggshell. Therefore, the ever-resourceful female mosquito works around this problem by taking the substances it needs from the blood of birds and mammals. This is why the female mosquito is more likely to bite during mosquito-breeding season than during any other time of the year.

Because it would be rare to find a male mosquito biting a human, it is rare to find a male mosquito that transmits the West Nile virus. However, it is interesting to ponder how a female mosquito "knows" that a particular component necessary for its eggs is in the blood of another animal. Most likely, evolution selected mosquitoes that produce protective coatings on the shells of their eggs. This means that the mosquitoes that, for some reason, fed on the blood of birds and mammals, were better able to survive and reproduce. However, the switch from a nectar-based diet to a blood meal is still a very intriguing curiosity. It raises the question why evolution did not select mosquitoes that are capable of generating their own protein to produce the protective shell of the egg. Consider what a different world we would live in if mosquitoes did not bite!

OUR BLOOD'S ABILITY TO CLOT SHOULD KILL A MOSQUITO

When a person or animal gets injured to the extent that the skin is broken and a blood vessel is torn, the body must rapidly repair itself to prevent severe blood loss that might eventually make the person or animal bleed to death. After injury occurs to a blood vessel, blood platelets (tiny fragments of cells that are part of the blood) bind around the wound to create a primary seal known as a hemostatic plug. The platelets then stimulate the formation of a secondary plug called a fibrin clot, which is made up of a protein called fibrin. These primary and secondary actions occur rapidly, although complete healing that includes new skin growth around the wound takes quite a bit more time, normally several days. This early process of healing is collectively known as blood coagulation (or clotting) and occurs within moments after the injury takes place.

When a mosquito feeds on the blood of an animal, the mosquito's mouth acts like a needle and pokes into the blood vessel of its host (Figure 5.1). This action of injecting the needle-like mouth (proboscis) into the vessel actually initiates blood coagulation. Normally, blood coagulation would prevent the mosquito from completing its meal because clots would rapidly form to heal the wound at the point in the skin where the mosquito has inserted its mouth. Additionally, the coagulated blood, which becomes very thick and viscous (having a sticky consistency), could potentially block the mosquito's mouth and prevent the mosquito from ever eating again. Thus, the mosquito's choice of a blood meal is potentially a life-threatening decision. Beyond the possibility of being slapped by the hand of its chosen host, the mosquito risks

Figure 5.1 A mosquito bite is actually the injection of the mosquito's needle-like mouth, or proboscis, into the host's blood vessel. The mosquito injects its saliva into the host, which contains a compound to prevent blood from clotting. Infected mosquitoes transmit West Nile virus when they bite. (© Christopher Badzioch/iStockphoto)

getting a blood clot that will block its throat and ultimately kill it. The mosquito avoids being slapped away by the host by producing an anesthetic that prevents the host from feeling the insertion of the mosquito's needle-like mouth. The mosquito also avoids the danger of blood clots by inhibiting blood coagulation through the production of a special anticoagulant (apyrase). Both of the compounds, the anesthetic and the anticoagulant, are found in the salivary glands of the mosquito. When a mosquito inserts its mouth into the skin of the host and finds a blood vessel, the mosquito immediately spits her saliva, which contains these compounds, into the blood vessel. This prevents the host's blood from clotting and allows the mosquito to suck the blood into its mouth. Unfortunately, if the mosquito is infected with a pathogen such as West Nile virus, the virus is injected along with the saliva into the host's blood, and the host becomes infected.

WHERE DO THE VIRUSES GO AFTER THEY ENTER THE BLOODSTREAM?

When a mosquito spits West Nile virus virions into the bloodstream of the host, the virus must seek out the first susceptible cell it can infect. At this point, a race between the replication cycle of the virus and the immune system of the host (Figure 5.2) begins. The virus tries to multiply as rapidly as possible, while the host's immune system tries to get rid of the virus before it kills too many host cells or before the host falls ill with a disease.

If the host has not been previously infected or immunized with a virus from the Flavivirus family, then the West Nile virus will likely have the advantage of entering the first cells without being detected by the immune system. Studies using mice and other laboratory rodents have indicated that the virus initially enters and begins replicating in the cells immediately surrounding the site of entry. These cells usually include Langerhans cells, which are **dendritic** cells found in the spaces between the cells of the epidermis (the outer layer of skin). Interestingly, Langerhans cells are cells of the immune system whose primary function is to process pathogens. However, the cells of the immune system are also the primary targets for virus replication.

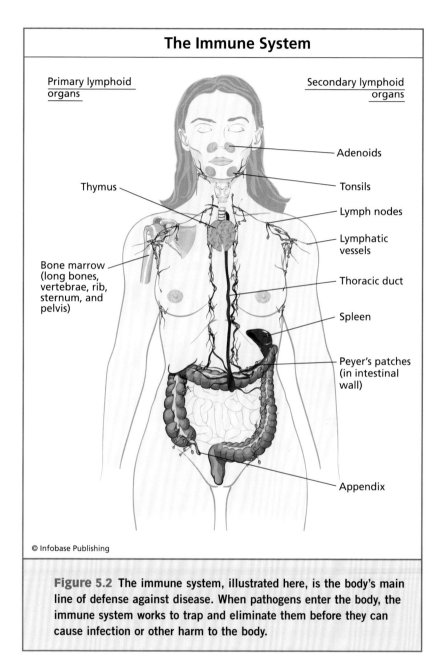

The Immune System

Primary lymphoid organs

Secondary lymphoid organs

Adenoids

Thymus

Tonsils

Lymph nodes

Lymphatic vessels

Bone marrow (long bones, vertebrae, rib, sternum, and pelvis)

Thoracic duct

Spleen

Peyer's patches (in intestinal wall)

Appendix

© Infobase Publishing

Figure 5.2 The immune system, illustrated here, is the body's main line of defense against disease. When pathogens enter the body, the immune system works to trap and eliminate them before they can cause infection or other harm to the body.

About one week after being infected by West Nile virus, the host launches an immune response that normally is effective in clearing the virus from the body. An immune response is mediated by B cells, which make antibodies—special proteins that will recognize the virus if it ever attacks again—and releases them into the bloodstream of the host. This response is normally very powerful in eliminating West Nile virus from the body. However, the precise timing of the body's immune response versus the accumulating numbers of replicating viruses is critical in determining how or whether the host will get sick.

WEST NILE VIRUS AND ENCEPHALITIS

The process by which West Nile virus and other flaviviruses acquire the ability to cause encephalitis is poorly understood, yet is crucial to our ability to prevent disease. After all, the main cause of death as a result of flavivirus infection comes from the replication and cellular damage in the brain and spinal cord. These cells are usually isolated from pathogens and chemicals of the bloodstream by a blockade of tight junctions of epithelical cells lining the blood vessels known as the blood-brain barrier (Figure 5.3). Only certain substances are able to cross the blood-brain barrier and directly affect the cells of the brain. When a substance—especially a pathogen like West Nile virus—crosses the blood-brain barrier and begins to infect the cells of the brain, it is very dangerous. It appears that West Nile virus's ability to break through the blood-brain barrier depends on viremia—how concentrated the virus is within the bloodstream. The higher the number of viruses in the body, the more likely it is that the virus will be able to attack brain cells.

From this correlation we could infer that the ability of the virus to cross the blood-brain barrier is an inefficient process that requires a frequency of attempts only produced by high viremia. Studies in mice have shown that **lesions** in the blood-brain barrier also help shuttle flaviviruses into the brain tissue. It is possible that the virus itself is capable of producing these lesions by infecting the cells that make up the vessel wall of the blood-brain barrier. Destruction of the cells that make up the blood-brain barrier would be an effective way to gain access to the vulnerable brain tissue. However, this ability to produce such a lesion has not been experimentally demonstrated to date.

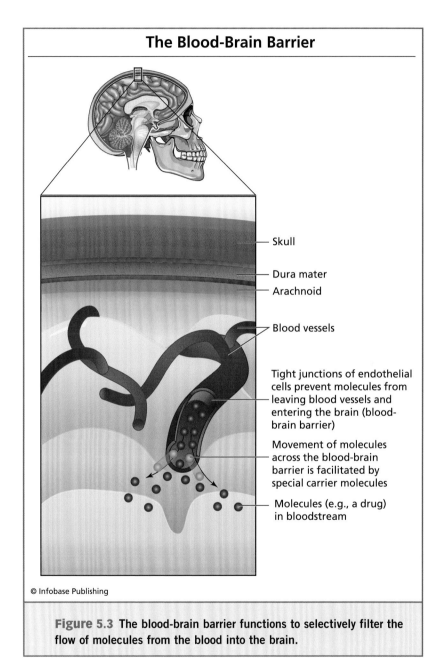

The Blood-Brain Barrier

Skull

Dura mater

Arachnoid

Blood vessels

Tight junctions of endothelial cells prevent molecules from leaving blood vessels and entering the brain (blood-brain barrier)

Movement of molecules across the blood-brain barrier is facilitated by special carrier molecules

Molecules (e.g., a drug) in bloodstream

© Infobase Publishing

Figure 5.3 The blood-brain barrier functions to selectively filter the flow of molecules from the blood into the brain.

Another way to gain access to brain tissue is a direct route through the olfactory system (the organs that relate to the sense of smell, i.e., the nose and sinus cavities). Spraying substances into the nose is a common method used in the laboratory to expose brain tissue to a particular substance. It has actually been reported that high concentrations of flaviviruses in labora-

INTERNATIONAL COMMITTEE ON THE TAXONOMY OF VIRUSES

At the turn of the 20th century, the first viruses were isolated and began to be characterized. Initially, viruses were simply described by their relatively small size, as determined by how easily they could be filtered. The study of viruses focused on their ability to cause infections and disease. By the 1930s, the study of viruses revealed differences in both the structure and composition of virions. Shortly after this conceptual advance, viruses were grouped into families based on these properties.

However, the limited knowledge of virus diversity did not provide for enough organization in the field. An explosion of newly discovered viruses in the 1950s led to chaos in classification schemes. Virologists (scientists who study viruses) everywhere understood that a single unifying method of organization had to be adopted in order to classify all these new viruses.

In 1966, the International Committee on the Taxonomy of Viruses (ICTV) was created at a meeting in Moscow, Russia. Initially, there were many arguments over which aspects of virology (the study of viruses) would be most important in the classification scheme. Based on these arguments, new viruses today are first classified based on their genetic composition, capsid symmetry, and the presence or absence of a lipid coat. Any changes to these classifications are made by the ICTV, which consists of 400 virologists from around the world. The ICTV has defined five orders, 84 families, and 314 genera for more than 3,600 virus species. Hundreds of viruses still remain unassigned, because there is not enough data on their characteristics. In addition, there are about 45,000 recorded virus names.

tory samples have been responsible for causing accidental fatal encephalitis in two scientists, which suggests that intranasal inoculation is a viable means of becoming infected with a flavivirus like West Nile. However, the extent to which natural West Nile virus infections of brain tissue use the olfactory route for access has not been determined. Such a mechanism of infection is not believed to be very likely.

Another means of developing encephalitis from exposure to the West Nile virus is associated with genetic mutation. Research with mice has shown that there is a host gene for susceptibility to West Nile virus.[1] In general, West Nile virus will cause encephalitis and death in most inbred laboratory mouse strains when they are inoculated with it. In one experiment, most of the strains of trapped wild mice were completely resistant to the virus.[2] Further investigation showed that a mutation existed on a gene located on chromosome number five that caused lab mice to be susceptible to the virus. The wild mice had a normal copy of this gene and were resistant to infection.

Several mechanisms have been identified for the crossing of the blood-brain barrier by West Nile virus. It has been suggested that the virus enters the brain via axonal transport through olfactory neurons. This means that inhaling the virus into the nose allows it to travel along the axons of the nerves that carry the sense of smell from the nose into the brain. Another route is the crossing of the blood-brain barrier via replication in vascular endothelial cells (cells that line the blood vessels that nourish the brain, particularly the capillaries) and release of virus into brain tissue. A third mechanism is diffusion of virus from vascular endothelial cells in situations where the blood-brain barrier is leaky due to damage from related or unrelated trauma.

Understanding the mechanism used by West Nile virus and other pathogens to cross the blood-brain barrier is of great importance, not only to microbiologists, but also to the pharmaceutical companies that work to design drugs that can effectively cross this barrier to help cure infections of the brain tissue. Preventing

West Nile virus from crossing the blood-brain barrier would most likely reduce its ability to cause fatal encephalitis.

THE DEATH OF A CELL

Viral pathogenesis is usually the result of the death or loss of function of important cells. This effect may be the direct consequence of the viral proteins or a type of cellular suicide brought on by the detection of a virus inside the cell. The virus may directly destroy a host cell through at least two methods.

One method used by many viruses involves exploding the cell after the virus has replicated itself and assembled new virions. Viruses that explode their host cells are known as lytic viruses, and they destroy the cell (through a process called **lysis**, Figure 5.4) in order to escape into the body of the host. Usually, these lytic viruses do not have any other way to get out of the cell they have infected, such as going through the secretory pathway, as West Nile virus does. Therefore, lytic viruses appear to fill the cell with new virions until the cell can no longer contain them. The overfilled cell then bursts and releases the viruses. This type of mechanism usually involves rapid replication and results in relatively short infection periods, since the cell used to replicate the virus is destroyed and cannot be used again to keep making more viruses.

Another mechanism involves debilitating the cell by stealing the cell's own proteins. Nucleic acids are translated into proteins by a **ribosome**. The virus may recruit all of the cell's ribosomes for the purpose of synthesizing viral proteins and leave very few left over to maintain the general health of the cell. This type of cellular death may also be induced by competition for other components of the host cellular machinery. For example, West Nile virus uses the membrane of the **endoplasmic reticulum** in its replication cycle. Although the endoplasmic reticulum is a flexible organelle that can increase or decrease in size depending on demand by the cell, if a virus overuses it, this is likely taxing on the cell's ability to stay alive.

The cell has evolved several defenses for fighting off viral infections. Some of these defenses target the virus's nucleic acids

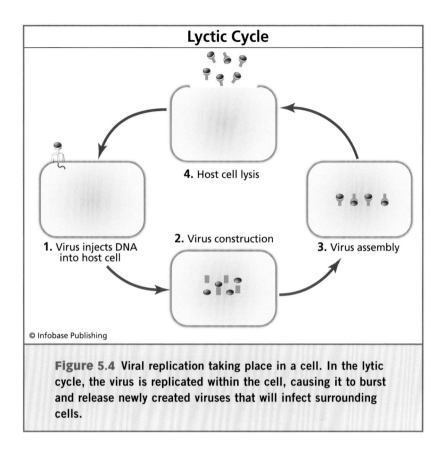

Lyctic Cycle

4. Host cell lysis

1. Virus injects DNA
into host cell

2. Virus construction

3. Virus assembly

© Infobase Publishing

Figure 5.4 Viral replication taking place in a cell. In the lytic cycle, the virus is replicated within the cell, causing it to burst and release newly created viruses that will infect surrounding cells.

and try to degrade or destroy them. If these mechanisms fail, then the cell may sacrifice itself in order to stop the infection and save the rest of the organism. This kind of self-sacrifice is known as **apoptosis** or programmed cell death (Figure 5.5). Apoptosis begins with the condensation of the cell's chromosomes and an overall shrinkage of the cell. The process, when induced in response to an infection, is intended to stop and contain the infection. The cell's plasma membrane remains intact throughout the entire process. Thus, the virus is not released, but is kept inside the cell, so that it dies along with the cell it has infected. While the membrane remains intact, protrusions known as membrane blebs ("blebs" are "blisters") are characteristic of an apoptotic cell (Figure 5.6). These blebs send out signals to macrophages, white blood cells that gobble up and remove dead

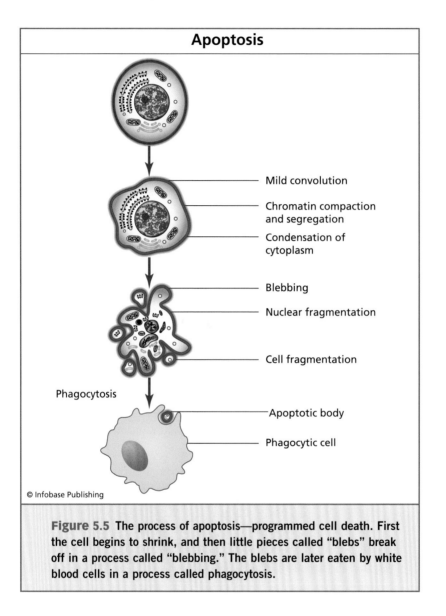

Apoptosis

Mild convolution

Chromatin compaction and segregation

Condensation of cytoplasm

Blebbing

Nuclear fragmentation

Cell fragmentation

Phagocytosis

Apoptotic body

Phagocytic cell

© Infobase Publishing

Figure 5.5 The process of apoptosis—programmed cell death. First the cell begins to shrink, and then little pieces called "blebs" break off in a process called "blebbing." The blebs are later eaten by white blood cells in a process called phagocytosis.

cells, telling them to remove the cell from the body. An apoptotic cell not only sends signals to macrophages to promote its own digestion, but also assists in its digestion by pinching off bits of itself that can be more easily engulfed by the macrophage. Ultimately, the virus that infected the cell and any additional viruses that were replicated inside the cell are destroyed. This process of cell death has consequences, however. Imagine that several cells in a region of the brain undergo apoptosis. Will these cells be missed after they are gone? If the "suicidal" cells have a vital function, they can cause severe harm to the body when they die. In

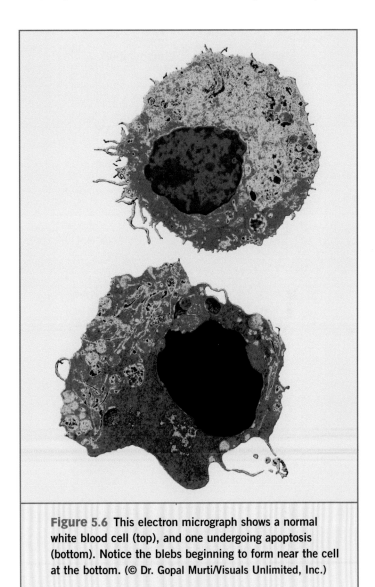

Figure 5.6 This electron micrograph shows a normal white blood cell (top), and one undergoing apoptosis (bottom). Notice the blebs beginning to form near the cell at the bottom. (© Dr. Gopal Murti/Visuals Unlimited, Inc.)

addition, scar tissue may also form in place of these cells, which produces lesions within the tissue and may disrupt the function of the organ of which the apoptotic cell was a part.

Table 5.1 West Nile case data by state for the year of 2008

State	Encephalitis/ Meningitis	Fever	Other Clinical/ Unspecified	Total	Fatalities
Alabama	11	7	0	18	0
Arizona	62	43	9	114	7
Arkansas	7	2	0	9	0
California	292	149	4	445	15
Colorado	17	54	0	71	1
Connecticut	5	2	1	8	0
Delaware	0	0	1	1	0
District of Columbia	4	1	3	8	0
Florida	3	0	0	3	0
Georgia	4	3	1	8	0
Idaho	2	31	6	39	1
Illinois	12	4	4	20	1
Indiana	3	0	1	4	0
Iowa	3	0	3	6	1
Kansas	14	17	0	31	0
Kentucky	3	0	0	3	0
Louisiana	18	31	0	49	1
Maryland	6	7	1	14	0
Massachusetts	1	0	0	1	0
Michigan	11	4	2	17	0
Minnesota	2	8	0	10	0
Mississippi	22	43	0	65	2
Missouri	12	3	0	15	1
Montana	0	3	2	5	0
Nebraska	7	40	0	47	1
Nevada	9	5	2	16	0

Apoptosis also occurs naturally without invasion by a virus. In these situations the process will lead to a positive outcome for the organism. An excellent example of this occurs during fetal

Table 5.1 (continued)

State	Encephalitis/ Meningitis	Fever	Other Clinical/ Unspecified	Total	Fatalities
New Jersey	6	4	0	10	2
New Mexico	5	3	0	8	0
New York	32	14	0	46	6
North Carolina	2	0	1	3	0
North Dakota	2	35	0	37	0
Ohio	14	1	0	15	1
Oklahoma	4	5	0	9	0
Oregon	3	13	0	16	0
Pennsylvania	12	2	0	14	1
Rhode Island	1	0	0	1	0
South Carolina	0	1	0	1	0
South Dakota	11	28	0	39	0
Tennessee	12	7	0	19	1
Texas	40	24	0	64	1
Utah	6	18	2	26	0
Virginia	0	0	1	1	0
Washington	2	1	0	3	0
West Virginia	1	0	0	1	0
Wisconsin	4	3	1	8	1
Wyoming	0	8	0	8	0
Totals	687	624	45	1356	44

Note: These numbers reflect both mild and severe human disease cases occurring between January 1, 2008 to December 31, 2008 as reported through April 10, 2009 to ArboNET by state and local health departments. ArboNET is the national, electronic surveillance system established by CDC to assist states in tracking West Nile virus and other mosquito-borne viruses.

Source: Centers for Disease Control and Prevention. http://www.cdc.gov/ncidod/dvbid/ westnile/surv&controlCaseCount08_detailed.htm.

development. As the hands and feet develop, the skin of the fingers and toes is connected. As apoptosis occurs in this skin, the cells die, thus allowing the digits to become separate from each other. The process also occurs every day in all humans. Billions of cells become old and can no longer divide by mitosis. When apoptosis occurs in these cells they will die and be removed to make way for new cells in the tissues. If the process does not occur as it is supposed to, too many cells may remain in an area leading to the development of tumors and even cancer.

Each of these processes described above may contribute to the **pathology** of West Nile virus infections. Lesions and **hemorrhages** have been found in the brains of birds infected with West Nile virus. Ultimately, it is the death or the inability of cells to perform their normal functions and the processes of clearing the virus from the body by the immune system that causes the disease associated with West Nile virus.

PATTERNS OF PATHOGENESIS

The flaviviruses induce encephalitis to varying degrees. Three categories of degrees of severity for the infection, or **patterns of pathogenesis**, have been described:

1. Fatal encephalitis

2. Subclinical encephalitis

3. Unapparent infection.

The most severe pattern of pathogenesis is fatal encephalitis, which is thought to occur when the virus rapidly replicates in the body of the host and accumulates to high viremia. The high viremia then infects the tissues of the brain, resulting in advanced encephalitis and death. A less severe pattern of pathogenesis is called subclinical encephalitis. The virus never achieves high viremia during subclinical encephalitis pathogenesis. Infection and replication in the neural tissues does occur, but results in minimal destruction of the brain tissue. The majority of West

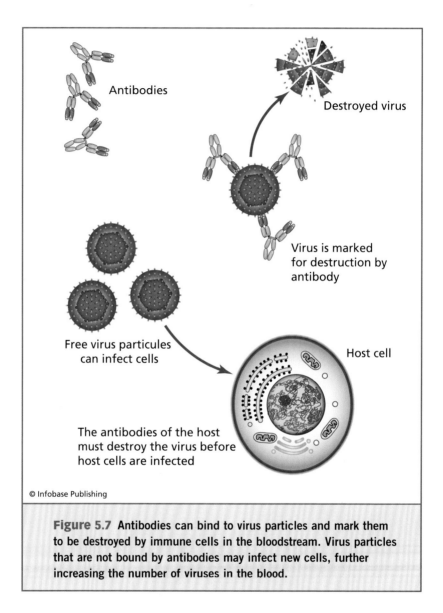

Antibodies

Destroyed virus

Virus is marked
for destruction by
antibody

Free virus particules
can infect cells

Host cell

The antibodies of the host
must destroy the virus before
host cells are infected

© Infobase Publishing

**Figure 5.7 Antibodies can bind to virus particles and mark them
to be destroyed by immune cells in the bloodstream. Virus particles
that are not bound by antibodies may infect new cells, further
increasing the number of viruses in the blood.**

Nile virus infections result in the third pattern of pathogenesis,
which is called unapparent infection. Only barely detectable viremia is achieved, and the virus does not infect the brain. A person
with an unapparent infection will probably never know that he

or she was ever infected with West Nile virus. Table 5.1 shows the pathogenesis of West Nile virus, tracing the number of cases by state in the year 2008.

The reasons why an infection of West Nile virus may result in fatal encephalitis in one person and unapparent infection in another person are not completely predictable, but have to do with several genetic, immunological, and virological variables. For example, some people's genetic profile may make them more vulnerable to West Nile virus than others. Evidence of such a genetic difference has been identified in mice. The presence of a particular gene in certain mice makes outcomes of West Nile infections more likely to result in subclinical encephalitis than in fatal encephalitis. The identity of this gene may be of importance to humans, since selective genetic pressures have shown patterns of pathogenesis in other viruses. A recent example is a genetic mutation that appears to make some people immune to HIV (human immunodeficiency virus; the virus that causes acquired immunodeficiency syndrome, or AIDS).

Genetic resistance to HIV occurs at two different levels. It appears that the strongest resistance to infection occurs in people with European or Central Asian heritage. Approximately 1 percent of those descended from Northern Europeans are immune to HIV infection, with Swedes showing the highest levels of protection. These people share a pair of mutated genes that prevent their helper T-lymphocytes from producing the necessary receptor for viral attachment to the cell. Without this receptor, the virus cannot enter the cell, replicate, and destroy it. If a person were to inherit the damaged gene from only one parent, he or she will have a greater resistance to infection by the virus than most people, but they won't be immune. Approximately 10 to 15 percent of people descended from Northern Europeans demonstrate this lesser degree of protection.

The ability of a host to rapidly develop neutralizing antibodies also results in differences in disease outcome. If a person's immune system is strong and healthy, then pathogens are quickly cleared from the body by strong antibody production. However, if genetic factors, age, or unhealthy lifestyles have weakened a person's ability to launch an effective immune response, then the person will be more likely to develop subclinical encephalitis or fatal encephalitis than an unapparent infection. Unfortunately, young children often have an underdeveloped immune system, which makes them more susceptible to the West Nile virus.

Two viral factors that may affect the pattern of pathogenesis are the rate at which mutations occur in the viral genome and the amount of the virus that is introduced into the body. Viruses are known to evolve over time. This evolution depends on two factors: the number of times a virus enters a cell of the infected host, and whether or not mistakes are made during the replication of the viral genome. The replication cycle of viruses occurs millions of times during an infection, and each time the genome is replicated, the virus has an opportunity to change, or mutate, its genetic material. The replication strategy of West Nile virus relies on acute infections in which viruses replicate themselves rapidly in the host, thus creating the greater potential to accumulate mutations by having as many replication events as possible. The other viral factor that affects pathogenesis patterning is the amount of virus that is first introduced into the host (viral load). An acute viral infection is a race between the virus replication cycle and the immune system. A small number of virions in the initial infection generally will take a longer amount of time to multiply to an infectious viremia than will an infection that started with thousands of virions. Thus, an infection that starts with a small number of virions will be more likely to be cleared by the immune system before disease sets in than an infection that starts with a higher initial number of virions. The pathogenesis patterning of West Nile virus infection correlates with the rapid replication of the virus within the host.

6

Diagnosis and Treatment of West Nile Virus Infections

Rachel had worked hard during college and graduate school to earn her doctorate and eventually become a medical laboratory director. Her passion was to help medical doctors diagnose unusual diseases and save lives. Her dedication and concern were about to pay off.

When the blood sample came into the health department lab where she worked, Rachel read the accompanying patient record carefully to determine which tests she needed to perform to diagnose the condition. She noted that the 73-year-old female was admitted suffering from typical symptoms of encephalitis: a severe headache, nausea, vomiting, a stiff neck, confusion, and irritability. Now, the question was, "Which of the many culprits is causing the condition?" There was also a note in the record that mentioned the discovery of two dead crows right outside of the patient's home. They too were sent to the lab for study.

She immediately began her quest for the answer by performing a diagnostic test on part of the blood sample. She would be looking for antibodies produced by the patient's immune system to combat a specific microorganism. When she determined that a virus was the cause of the symptoms, she knew that in order for the doctors to properly treat the patient, they had to know exactly which virus was involved.

Rachel also took two brain tissue samples from the birds and sent one over to the electron microscopy department so that they might be able to visualize the virus. The other sample was sent to the genetics lab and to the Centers for Disease Control in Atlanta, Georgia, so that both labs could perform genetic sequencing to accurately identify the virus that was causing the encephalitis.

She wrote up her report and got it back to the treating phy-sicians as soon as she could so they could begin treatment right away. Of course, they would have to wait for the results from the other labs as well, but they could begin symptomatic treatment of the patient in an effort to save her life.

Viruses are often the most difficult illnesses to diagnose accurately, and they are impossible to cure. Virus infections are often short-lived, lasting only a few days, and have the same general symptoms—such as headache, fatigue, and fever—as bacterial infections. However, when a viral infection overcomes the defense systems of the host's body, the disease that results can be fatal. Populations at risk of fatal infections, especially people with compromised immune systems or elderly and very young people, require rapid responses to diagnose and combat the virus before it proves lethal.

DIAGNOSIS OF THE WEST NILE VIRUS

Diagnoses of the first cases of West Nile virus in New York during the summer of 1999 were the most difficult because the virus had not historically posed a threat to the region. Therefore, the physicians who saw the first patients were caught completely off guard. When the doctors identified the symptoms of encephalitis in the seven human cases that summer, the first things that researchers wanted to know was whether a common infectious agent was involved. If there were a common infectious agent, was it a bacterium or a virus? A **bacterium** is a free-living, single-celled organism. A **virus** is a parasite of plants, animals, and bacteria, and is not always considered a living organism because it is unable to reproduce itself without a host cell. Since encephalitis is most commonly caused by viral infections and because the first patients did not respond to treatments of antibiotics, which are generally able to stop bacterial infections, the physicians deduced that the cause was most likely a virus.

The next questions that had to be answered were *which* virus was causing the disease and *how* it was being transmitted.

Scientists have developed several techniques to precisely identify most of the known viruses and they understand the steps that need to be taken to identify new viruses. These tests include detecting whether the virus reacts to specific antibodies, using a microscope to determine the shape of the virus, and sequencing the genetic code of the virus. Each of these techniques has different levels of sensitivity and they are normally used in a progressive order to determine the virus's identity.

ELISA

The first and most commonly used diagnostic test is known as an ELISA, or **enzyme-linked immunosorbent assay** test, and has been made easily available to physicians through commercial companies. The test takes advantage of antibodies, which are generated by the body's immune system response to the proteins of the infectious agent at the start of an infection. These protein targets are known as antigens. Antibodies bind to the antigen and mark it for destruction by the host. To achieve this destruction of the infectious agent, antibodies must be highly specific to the targeted antigen. If they lack specificity, a signal for destruction may be generated against the host organism itself, a process that is known as autoimmune disease, in which the body actually attacks its own cells. The ELISA test takes advantage of the antibody's specificity and allows rapid detection of a variety of antigens that may be similar to those present in a patient's blood or tissue. The test involves applying a small drop of blood serum to a vessel that has antigens from various infectious agents attached to its walls. If a patient's serum has an antibody that is specific for an antigen that is present in the vessel, the antibody remains tightly bound to the antigen even when the solution is rinsed out of the well. Antibodies bound to the antigen are then discovered by using an enzyme that detects the antibody-antigen complex. When the enzyme solution is added to the well, a change in the color of the solution indicates that the patient has antibodies to the antigen in that well and has probably been infected with the agent that produces the antigen (Figure 6.1).

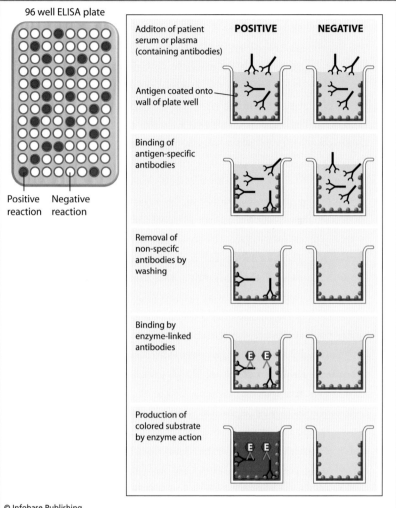

96 well ELISA plate

Positive   Negative
reaction   reaction

Additon of patient serum or plasma (containing antibodies)

POSITIVE   **NEGATIVE**

Antigen coated onto wall of plate well

Binding of antigen-specific antibodies

Removal of non-specifc antibodies by washing

Binding by enzyme-linked antibodies

Production of colored substrate by enzyme action

© Infobase Publishing

Figure 6.1 An **ELISA (enzyme-linked immunosorbent assay)** is one test used to determine if West Nile virus is present in a person's blood. A sample of the person's serum is placed in wells on a glass or plastic plate. These wells have already been treated with antigens for the infectious agent for which the test is being done. The serum is allowed to incubate in the wells and is then washed out. If the serum sample contains antibodies to the pathogen, they will stick to the wells when the serum is removed. Next, a solution containing a special marker is added to the wells. It will react with the antigen-antibody complex (if present) and change color.

Wide arrays of ELISA tests are available to physicians and veterinarians. Virus-specific ELISA tests from the serum of the initial cases of encephalitis were performed by the New York City Department of Health to start the investigation of the encephalitis cases. Blood samples were also submitted to the Centers for Disease Control and Prevention (CDC), whose branch in Fort Collins, Colorado, holds the facilities for the diagnosis of vector-borne infectious diseases. The hopes were that the CDC might identify which of the viruses known to exist in the United States was the cause of this outbreak. Though the initial diagnosis of St. Louis encephalitis was incorrect, the misidentification allowed the encephalitis cases to be correctly labeled as arbovirus encephalitis. Previous outbreaks of St. Louis encephalitis virus had been reported in the United States and it was known that mosquitoes transmit the virus to humans. Therefore, the CDC initiated mosquito control measures in northern Queens and the South Bronx, where the first six cases of encephalitis had been identified.

Just weeks after the ELISA tests were ordered for the human specimens, another battery of ELISA tests was being processed on samples from birds that had died at the Bronx Zoo. These tests were performed at the National Veterinary Services Laboratory (NVSL) in Ames, Iowa. The NVSL used an ELISA test similar to that performed on the blood from the people who had encephalitis. However, this ELISA was specific for common bird pathogens and was surprisingly negative for a reaction to each of the antigens. The pathology of the dead birds indicated that their death was viral-related, but that the virus was not a pathogen that was common to birds in the northeastern United States.

MICROSCOPY

The unidentified virus from one of the birds was then put through a more rigorous, but also more expensive and time-consuming, method of identification through microscopy. Virus particles were isolated from the bird's tissue and then

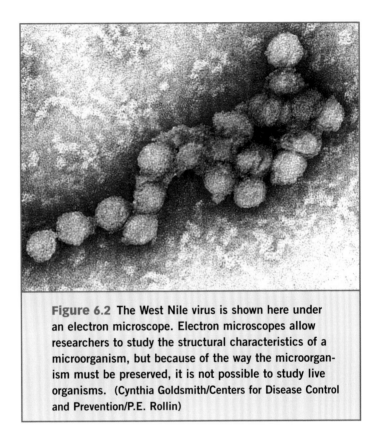

Figure 6.2 The West Nile virus is shown here under an electron microscope. Electron microscopes allow researchers to study the structural characteristics of a microorganism, but because of the way the microorganism must be preserved, it is not possible to study live organisms. (Cynthia Goldsmith/Centers for Disease Control and Prevention/P.E. Rollin)

further amplified by injecting the particles into chicken eggs. The technique of using chicken eggs to grow viruses is common in virology laboratories to produce large quantities of virus for further experimentation. A portion of the concentrated virus grown in the chicken eggs was analyzed with a high-powered microscope. Determining the shape of the infectious agent often helps indicate that the culprit is, indeed, a virus and not a bacterium. Bacteria are much larger than viruses and may not have an ordered structure like a virus does. The shape and size of a virus may also give an indication of the virus family of which a particular virus is a member.

Viruses are extremely small compared to most bacteria. A single infected cell can contain thousands of virus particles.

Thus, visualization of these particles requires an extremely high-magnification microscope known as an electron microscope. Electron microscopes fire a stream of electrons at an object to reveal its structural characteristics (Figure 6.2). When these images are generated, they often provide information about interactions between the virus and the cells. However, producing electron microscope images requires preservation of the samples, which can be difficult and is often not practical for rapid processing, especially during a routine visit to the doctor's office.

GENETIC SEQUENCING

Another portion of the concentrated virus was then sent to the CDC in Fort Collins, Colorado, for identification. The genome of the viral DNA was determined using robotic sequencing methods. The sequence of the virus genome was then compared to a database of known viral genomes. This comparative analysis revealed that the virus was closely related to West Nile virus, which had first been discovered in the West Nile Province of Uganda. In fact, the viruses isolated from the Bronx Zoo flamingo in New York, now known as "West Nile virus New York 1999" or "WN-NY99," was more than 99.8 percent similar to a West Nile virus isolated in Israel in 1998, known as "WN-Israel 1998." Only two positions out of the 1,278 positions in the genetic code that were sequenced turned out to be different. A similar genomic analysis at the CDC identified West Nile virus in a brain tissue sample from one of the people who had been diagnosed with fatal encephalitis in New York that same year. After the complete analysis was performed, it was determined that the WN-Israel 1998 virus was greater than 99 percent similar to viruses isolated around New York in 1999 from human brain, mosquitoes, and birds. These tests provided the first definitive evidence that West Nile virus was in the United States. The West Nile virus–specific test is now used as the gold standard in the detection of West Nile virus infections and is commonly used in the United States.

TREATMENTS FOR WEST NILE VIRUS INFECTIONS

Before the outbreak of human immunodeficiency virus (HIV) in the United States, there were only a handful of drugs available that were specifically designed to combat viral infections. Since the advent of the AIDS epidemic in the early 1980s, however, funding for virus research by both government agencies and private institutions has rapidly advanced our understanding of viruses and aided in the development of new drugs to help prevent viruses from replicating. However, the drugs we have today are still not effective for stopping the replication cycle of West Nile virus. One reason that they do not work for West Nile virus is that current drugs were not designed to attack the specific proteins of the virus. In theory, some of the conceptual targets of the drugs designed to attack other viruses could be altered to work against West Nile virus, but another problem exists. The replication cycle and the onset of diseases caused by West Nile virus are much faster than for viruses that are currently considered treatable. West Nile virus can cause fatal encephalitis within just days, whereas a person may be infected with HIV for as long as a decade before disease sets in. This short window of opportunity for treating West Nile virus is a severe problem for drug development.

For the reasons outlined above, there are currently no specific therapies for people infected with West Nile virus. In the case of serious illnesses caused by the virus, physicians are recommended to provide intensive support therapy, which may involve hospitalization, intravenous (IV) fluids (provided through a needle inserted into a vein), use of a ventilator to assist breathing, medications to control seizures, brain swelling, nausea and vomiting, and the use of antibiotics to prevent bacterial infections from making the disease even worse.

7

Vaccines and Prevention

Vaccination refers to the introduction of a potentially disease-causing substance into the body to produce immunity to a disease. It has been the pinnacle of infectious disease prevention and treatment for the last century. The development of **vaccines** against many diseases has helped essentially eradicate certain pathogens from the planet, such as the smallpox virus and the poliovirus. However, vaccine development is not easy or simple. A vaccine must be both safe for the person receiving it and effective at conferring immunity to disease. Additionally, financial considerations must be addressed in manufacturing a vaccine. If a vaccine is expected to be used to wipe out a disease among a large population, then huge quantities of the vaccine must be available for a very low cost. At least two U.S. companies—Acambis and Fort Dodge—have weighed the costs and probability for success, and have stepped up to the challenge of creating a vaccine for West Nile virus.

WHY DEVELOP A VACCINE
AGAINST WEST NILE VIRUS NOW?

Outbreaks of West Nile virus have been reported and documented since 1937. Why hasn't a vaccine been developed yet? The answer to this question is surprisingly straightforward from several viewpoints. Most importantly, until recently, outbreaks of West Nile virus were simply not as severe as they have been since the 1999 outbreak. Previous outbreaks rarely caused fatal encephalitis in humans and those people who did become infected were able to develop immunity to the disease. However, the strain that appeared in the United States in 1999 seems to be particularly virulent. During the 1999 outbreak, several people died of West Nile virus.

Santa Clara County Library District
Checkout Receipt
11/07/2015 2:47 PM

24/7 Renewals:
Online at www.sccl.org
Telecirc: 800-471-0991

Patron ID: p10759359

West Nile virus / Jeffrey Sfakianos and
33305221577582   DUE: **11-28-15**

Thank you for visiting the library!

In addition, the frequency of outbreaks before 1999 was sparse. Only eight outbreaks were reported during the 45 years prior to 1995. However, this number of reported outbreaks was matched over the following five years, from 1996 to 2000. Thus, both the frequency and severity of outbreaks are on the rise for West Nile virus.

According to the U.S. Centers for Disease Control and Prevention, the West Nile virus infected nearly 175,000 people last year.[1] The virus caused serious diseases such as encephalitis and meningitis in 1,227 people, caused nearly 35,000 cases of fever, and killed 117 people in 2007. As of December 31, 2008, the CDC reported a total of 2,356 cases of the virus nationwide with 44 fatalities.[2]

Other factors have also influenced the demand for vaccine development. Since the *Culex* mosquito prefers to breed in man-made structures like birdbaths and garbage cans, the disease is prevalent in both affluent neighborhoods and urban cities. The residents of these neighborhoods demand that the government and medical professionals take action against threats such as West Nile virus, and their demands are fueled by local media coverage through newspapers, television, and radio. Furthermore, West Nile virus has spread to new places each year since the 1999 outbreak in New York. Neglecting such obvious signs to cut off the spread of the virus to new areas would simply be irresponsible.

Unfortunately, actions toward preventing or treating the West Nile virus disease haven't been easy to identify or implement. Drugs designed to target the replication cycle of viruses have experienced a surge in development over the last decade thanks to new technologies, but most of the efforts have been directed toward finding treatments for patients infected with HIV. In part, the application of new technologies to HIV research is justified, since infections by this virus are long-term and almost invariably fatal. A person infected with HIV may have detectable viremia for decades, which is usually

EDWARD JENNER'S VACCINATION

Edward Jenner (1749–1823) (Figure 7.1) was trained as a physician in London, England. After his training, Jenner enlisted in the army as a surgeon. However, it was not in either of these two roles that Edward Jenner performed his revolutionary work. Jenner changed the world by providing the tools to eradicate the scourge of smallpox. At the time, smallpox was a devastating virus that was usually fatal to the people it infected, most of whom were infants and young children. Jenner had a superb reputation as a physician in the small town of Gloucestershire in the west of England during the time that smallpox was prevalent. One of his observations was that milkmaids seemed to be resistant to smallpox. The milkmaids often got a milder version of the disease that is known as cowpox, which causes blisters to form on the hands. Jenner made a connection between the pus that oozed from the milkmaids' blisters and the women's resistance to smallpox. Luckily for James Phipps, Jenner's prediction was correct. After James was injected with pus from a cowpox blister several times, the young boy was exposed to a live sample of smallpox. The boy became mildly ill, but then recovered fully. In 1840, the English government made Jenner's vaccine the only legal form of treatment for the disease. Today the smallpox virus has been eradicated from the world. The word Jenner invented for his treatment, *vaccination*, (from the Latin "vacca" meaning cow) has come to refer to immunization against any disease.

associated with a chronic wasting disease, in which a person loses weight and muscle mass, even if he or she eats enough. Other viruses, on the other hand, such as influenza and flaviviruses like West Nile, are usually short-term infections that can only occasionally be fatal, with the illness often lasting for as few as 10 days. In the case of influenza, the onset of

Figure 7.1 Edward Jenner. (National Library of Medicine)

symptoms such as headache, fatigue, and fever is usually followed by a decline of viremia. Thus, drugs created to target the virus are only effective if they are used as a prevention of infection in the first place—not as a cure once infection has already occurred. The rapid and predictable spread of influenza virus during flu season through the well-defined at-risk population makes use of such a preventative agent. People who feel they have a high risk of exposure to influenza may decide to take the antiviral drugs for a period of time to prevent the infection from taking hold.

The West Nile virus, however, differs from the influenza virus in important ways. First, the spread of West Nile virus is not predictable, but random. Although certain populations are more likely to develop encephalitis due to infection than others, it is impossible to predict who will be bitten by an infected mosquito. Additionally, the actual number of human West Nile virus infections each year is far lower than the incidence of influenza, making preventative therapy for entire populations an inefficient prospect.

MOSQUITO CONTROL

One prophylactic (preventative) measure that has been effective in reducing human infections has been mosquito control. Local and state governments have sprayed chemicals around ponds and water sources that kill the mosquitoes (Figure 7.5). This prevents the amplification of West Nile virus in both the bird and mosquito population. However, this treatment also has critics, since the chemicals used to destroy the mosquitoes inevitably have unintended effects on humans and the environment.

On September 10, 2008, the Nassau County, New York, Department of Health ordered aerial spraying of the pesticide Scourge (Aventis Environmental Science) due to the highest West Nile virus-associated death rate in the history of the county. The pesticide was dropped over the county[3] from small planes beginning at 6:30 p.m, the time at which most adult mosquitoes are flying, thus increasing the probability that they would be exposed to the spray.

Scourge is a pesticide designed to be used outdoors. Its primary ingredients are resmethrin, an insecticide designed to kill adult mosquitoes, and piperonyl butoxide, a chemical that enhances the ability of resmethrin to kill mosquitoes.[4] It is possible that short-term exposure to the spray may cause affects on the human nervous system such as tremors, loss of coordination, or numbness and tingling. The compound is also listed as being possibly carcinogenic (cancer-causing). The spray is toxic to fish and bees and should be avoided by pregnant women and children. For these reasons, the public was notified to stay indoors during the spraying and for 30 minutes afterward, to cover swimming pools and children's toys, and to keep doors and windows closed and turn off air conditioners. Health experts agree, however, that at the low levels of exposure, people are at little risk.

Negative side effects have been produced by pesticides in the past. For instance, the chemical pesticide DDT was used to save the lives of a billion people from malaria during the 1950s through the 1970s. However, it was later found that DDT, once present in the body's fat cells, is expected to stay in a person's body for the rest of his or her life. DDT was subsequently banned from use by order of the U.S. Environmental Protection Agency (EPA). Today, it is believed that no living organism is free of DDT contamination. The future use of pesticides is likely to suffer from guilt by association due to the history of DDT. Thus, although mosquito control through pesticide use is moderately effective at reducing the spread of West Nile virus, other techniques that have fewer environmental side effects would likely be more desirable and acceptable to the general public.

VACCINE RESEARCH
Live Attenuated Vaccines
The yellow fever virus vaccine is one of the most effective vaccines available and also the basis of the state-of-the-art vaccine development for current flavivirus vaccines. The yellow fever vaccine was developed from an isolated strain of yellow fever virus that was "passaged" in cell cultures many times, which eventually selects for a virus that causes less cell death. The

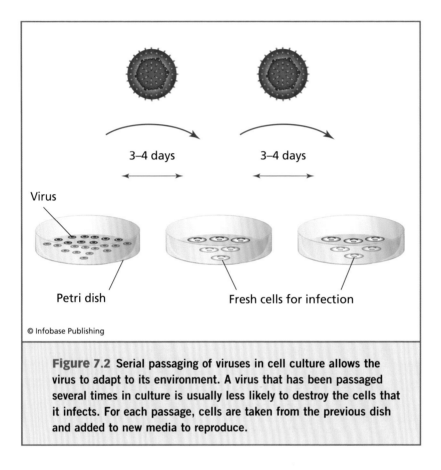

Virus

Petri dish   Fresh cells for infection

© Infobase Publishing

Figure 7.2 Serial passaging of viruses in cell culture allows the virus to adapt to its environment. A virus that has been passaged several times in culture is usually less likely to destroy the cells that it infects. For each passage, cells are taken from the previous dish and added to new media to reproduce.

process of passaging involves infecting cells that have been grown on a dish containing an artificial liquid medium used to feed the cells; in the case of the yellow fever vaccine, chicken cells were used.

The virus is allowed to replicate in these cells and expand into the medium as the replication cycle is completed. The new virions from the medium are used to infect a fresh plate of cells and the process is repeated (Figure 7.2). The process relies on chance that is facilitated by the error-prone replication cycle of the virus. Through the passaging process, the virus accumulates mutations. In the case of the yellow fever vaccine, the virus was passaged 204 times, meaning that a single virus was used to infect chicken cells and then the medium from these cells was used to infect fresh chicken cells 203 more times. The resulting virus had 61 nucleotide mutations that resulted in 31 amino acid changes.

The mutations caused the virus to become **attenuated**, meaning that it has reduced virulence but still has the ability to provoke a strong immune response. When a dose of yellow fever vaccine is given to a person, the virus replicates and induces an initial immune response usually within about five days. The induced immunity protects against yellow fever infections for more than 10 years. Booster vaccines are recommended every 10 years for people at continued risk of exposure.

Although the yellow fever vaccine has proven to be a model of safety and efficacy for vaccine development, and has been used to vaccinate more than 400 million people worldwide, the use of live attenuated virus vaccines comes with some inherent risk and is not the method of choice today. The risk that is always present in an attenuated virus is that the virus could continue to mutate and revert to its virulent form.

CURRENT DEVELOPMENT OF WEST NILE VIRUS VACCINES

Companies have built on the success of the yellow fever vaccine and advances in molecular biology to create what are called **chimera** viruses. Chimera viruses consist of components from different viruses that are combined into a single virus. The resulting virus should have the desired properties of each individual virus. This technology for vaccine design, which has been trademarked under the name ChimeriVax in 2006 became the first veterinary vaccine for West Nile virus marketed under the name PreveNile. The vaccine is used on horses in a single dose. (Figure 7.3).

The technology uses much of the yellow fever virus genome, while replacing the antigenic proteins with those of West Nile virus. In particular, the untranslated terminal regions, the C protein, and the nonstructural proteins of yellow fever virus are

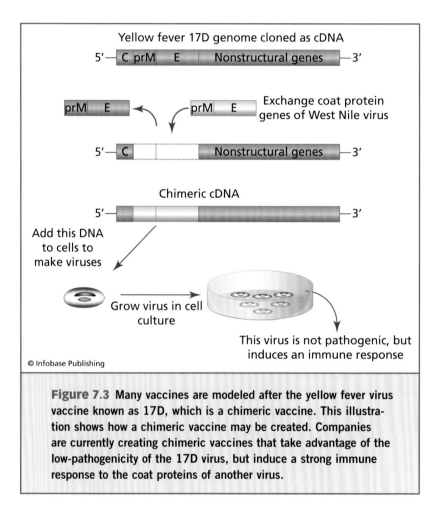

Figure 7.3 Many vaccines are modeled after the yellow fever virus vaccine known as 17D, which is a chimeric vaccine. This illustration shows how a chimeric vaccine may be created. Companies are currently creating chimeric vaccines that take advantage of the low-pathogenicity of the 17D virus, but induce a strong immune response to the coat proteins of another virus.

left intact and remain unchanged. The M and E proteins from West Nile virus are used in place of those for yellow fever virus. Chimera virus vaccines combine the efficacy and safety of the yellow fever vaccine with an immune response to the proteins of the West Nile virus. This is a logical approach, since most of the immune responses that are induced by a naturally occurring infection are targeted to the M and E proteins. Additionally, some antibodies to these proteins have proven to neutralize the virus, even in passive immunity procedures. Thus, a West

Nile virus vaccine based on ChimeriVax technology provides the best means to prevent the spread of the disease in the human population, especially if the vaccine is able to provide the same degree of protection as the parent vaccine provided for yellow fever virus.

Another promising technology for West Nile virus vaccine development is DNA vaccines. These types of vaccines typically introduce a subset of genes, or a single gene, into an organism. A strong advantage of this type of vaccine is the simplicity and economical production of vast quantities of vaccine doses. When injected into cells, the gene is expressed and presented to the immune system, which recognizes and reacts to it. Since the other proteins of the virus are not expressed, a virus that is able to replicate is not necessarily assembled. Thus, the probability of generating a safe vaccine is greater than when a live attenuated virus is used. However, preliminary data indicates that multiple doses may be required to induce the needed response to create lasting immunity. Additionally, delivery of DNA vaccines is sometimes daunting. Special equipment, such as a gene gun, may be necessary to deliver the DNA vaccine to cells.

In May 2008, associate professor Alex Khromykh, from Australia University of Queensland School of Molecular and Microbial Sciences, announced that he and his team successfully created a DNA vaccine that is safer, purer, and more stable than traditionally prepared vaccines.[5] The vaccine is called pKUNdC/C and utilizes an Australian subtype of the West Nile virus that appeared in New York in 1999. The virus, Kunjin (KUN), shares 98.5 percent of the amino acid structure with the New York virus. However, it is nonfatal and rarely causes disease in humans.

Khromykh found that a single gene-gun immunization with an extremely small amount of pKUNdC/C DNA was sufficient to bring about an excellent immune response able to completely protect animals against lethal challenge with the New York virus. The vaccine was tested on both mice and horses. It is felt that the vaccine is a highly efficient candidate against West Nile infection and is much better than other non-infectious DNA vaccine candidates.

As a result of Khromykh's successful research, Replikun Biotech Pty Limited, an Australian vaccine and immunotherapy company, has completed a license agreement with the University of Queensland to become responsible for all further development and commercialization of the vaccine. They are confident that a vaccine will now be developed in a much shorter period of time.

Using West Nile virus vaccines on horses is not a new concept. In August 2001, a vaccine for West Nile virus was approved by the U.S. Department of Agriculture and by the Department of Environmental Management of Rhode Island.[6] It was made available for sale to veterinarians in the state. The vaccine was manufactured by Fort Dodge Laboratories of Iowa.

Horses may commonly become infected with West Nile virus and show some typical signs of viral encephalitis. These include depression, stumbling, hind limb weakness, partial paralysis, incoordination, and muscle twitching. The symptoms are not exclusive to West Nile virus and a definitive diagnosis must be made after symptoms appear.

The $25 billion horse show and racing industry suffers greatly from West Nile virus infections. Horses are another favorite source of blood meals for mosquitoes and seem to be especially susceptible to encephalitis. Therefore, the horse industry strongly relies on a veterinary vaccine for West Nile virus. With luck, a successful vaccine for West Nile virus will serve both horses and humans equally. A vaccine that is economical and easy to distribute provides the best means to protect large populations against the virus, with the fewest undesirable side effects.

SURVEILLANCE OF WEST NILE VIRUS IN THE UNITED STATES

Surveillance of an infectious disease is absolutely necessary for effective prevention of the vectors that cause that disease. Sur-

GENE GUNS

A gene gun is exactly what its name implies, a gun that shoots genes into a cell. Designed by scientists at Cornell University, the gun's intended use was to introduce recombinant (genetically engineered) DNA into plants. The gun uses a burst of helium gas to propel DNA attached to metal balls into a cell. The metal balls are usually made of gold or tungsten and are only one micrometer in diameter. These tiny metal balls are shot from the gene gun at approximately the same speed as a bullet from a real gun. However, the small size of the balls does much less damage to body tissue than a bullet. The gene gun design has recently been re-engineered to include an electrical charge that helps the particles remain evenly dispersed. Thus, the damage caused by the tiny metal balls is reduced even more.

veillance data on West Nile virus help local health departments use resources in the proper locations and direct their efforts at the correct species of mosquitoes, which results in the fewest side effects and least contamination of the environment. The local health department is involved in organizing and monitoring the data on West Nile virus through bird deaths, human infections, and mosquito samples from different geographical locations. This information is then converted into public service announcements that are intended to alert the public of the proper precautions to take during periods of heightened risk of West Nile virus infection.

The high mortality rate of the American strains of West Nile virus infections in birds provides a surprising mode of surveillance that was not present in the European outbreaks of the virus. Since the West Nile virus entered the United States in 1999, the crow has emerged as an effective and easy-to-report surveillance tool. Unlike most of the European outbreaks of West Nile virus, the 1999 New York strain seems to be particularly virulent. In previous outbreaks, a bird's infection was more similar to an infection in humans—few birds died of the disease. However, the American hooded crow seems to be especially susceptible to West Nile virus. Dead crows have become a symbol for the presence of West Nile virus in a region.

Although the 1999 outbreak of West Nile virus in New York affected crows almost exclusively, to date the virus has been identified in more than 300 species of birds found dead in the United States. Most of these birds were identified based on reports made by the public to various health departments.

During the height of a West Nile virus outbreak, local health departments will ask people to report the location and species of any dead birds they see. Any person can and should participate in these local surveillance efforts. People can easily find out how to report this information by visiting their local health department's Web site and looking for information on West Nile virus. Links to state and local government West Nile virus Web sites can be found on the Centers for Disease Control and Prevention (CDC) Web site as well.

The CDC has created five categories of guidelines for the action that a local health department should take based on surveillance data. All categories recommend control of mosquito larvae, no matter what the risk is to humans. When mosquitoes are not breeding, the category is defined as 0 and there is "no risk" of human infection with West Nile virus.

When the mosquito-breeding season starts, an area that has had previous West Nile virus activity is changed to category 1, which predicts a "remote risk" of infection for humans. The CDC recommends that local health departments in category 1 counties use **larvicides**, chemicals that destroy the larval stage of an insect, and start collecting surveillance data on bird deaths and mosquitoes that carry the West Nile virus.

Once West Nile virus is detected during mosquito-breeding season, the category of the county is changed to 2, which indicates a "low risk" of infections for humans. The detection method that initiates the change to category 2 may be a dead bird reported by a local resident or detection of the **epizootic cycle** by random environmental testing of mosquitoes. The CDC recommends that local health departments in category 2 counties continue with the lower-level recommendations of action, while also beginning the use of adult mosquito pesticides, known as **adulticides**. In addition, the local health department should begin to alert the public that West Nile virus is in the area and should advise people to begin using personal protective measures, such as wearing insect repellent when spending time outdoors. The alerts could come from news releases issued by the health department, from the health department's Web site, or from newspaper advertisements, posters, or organized neighborhood discussions.

Once a horse or a human is confirmed to be infected with West Nile virus, the category of the county is increased to 3, which poses a "moderate risk" for further human infections. Additional actions recommended under category 3 are increased community outreach and intensified mosquito control.

Similar recommendations are issued for category 4 counties, which pose a "high risk" of human infection. Category 4 counties exhibit an increase in the density of bird deaths and also represent areas that have high numbers of infected mosquitoes that are identified by multiple tests.

MOSQUITO ELIMINATION

The ability of the CDC and local health departments to intervene in the course of a West Nile virus epidemic is somewhat limited. The primary tools of these agencies are mosquito control and increased public awareness, and the effective use of these tools relies on surveillance data. Moreover, the surveillance data must justify the use of chemical mosquito control measures before such actions may be used. The use of pesticides is always accompanied by some risk of unintended side effects and is expensive for the governing body to administer. Therefore, the use of pesticides should be considered carefully and the type of pesticide applied accurately.

Under these defined criteria, the most effective mosquito pesticide targets the larval stage of the mosquito life cycle. If a region of West Nile virus activity has been detected and confirmed, health officials can choose from a variety of larvicides, including chemicals (an organophosphate called temephos), bacteria that destroy the larvae (*Bacillus thuringiensis israelensis* and *Bacillus sphaericus*), larvicidal oils, or monomolecular surface films. Monomolecular surface films are interesting agents that cause the larvae to lose surface tension with the water source in which they are growing (Figure 7.4). The larvae then sink to the bottom of the pool and drown. Each of these formulations—whether chemical, biological, or oil-based—provide different degrees of specificity for targeting the mosquito larvae. However, each is considered to have fewer side effects on the environment than agents used to target the adult mosquito.

Figure 7.4 Mosquitoes lay their eggs in water, and the larvae grow hanging into the water, as seen in this photograph. One way to combat mosquitoes that spread disease is to kill them in this larval stage by using chemicals that break the surface tension on which they support themselves, making them sink and drown. (© Nancy Nehring/iStockphoto)

Figure 7.5 A worker sprays larvicide in an attempt to reduce the mosquito population. Many cities and states have taken measures such as this to protect people from diseases transmitted by mosquitoes, such as West Nile virus. (© AP Images)

Adulticides are generally applied by an apparatus that sprays an ultra-low volume of the substance into the air. To be killed, the adult mosquito must fly through the adulticide drifting in the air. This means that the application must be

Figure 7.6 Planes are used to spray pesticide over areas with mosquitoes carrying West Nile virus. (© AP Images)

applied during times of high mosquito activity. For the *Culex* species, this is usually in the late afternoon or evening hours. Thus, the adulticide must be sprayed during hours that are not generally part of the normal working day and must cover a large amount of geographic area.

The most effective means to control the mosquito population is to control the mosquito larval habitat (Figure 7.6).

This is collectively referred to as "source reduction." The health department should conduct water management on a large scale. Specific techniques have been developed for large sources of standing water such as marshes, dams, and storm water structures. These types of water sources may be periodically flooded to allow the bodies to serve ecological functions, but then drained prior to the completion of a full season of mosquito breeding. These techniques are not easily performed and require professional design and implementation. Source reduction on a small scale cannot be practically applied by the health department, but can be performed by individuals.

SOURCE REDUCTION BY INDIVIDUALS

One known fact that is instrumental in mosquito control is that the *Culex* species is a container breeder. Being a container breeder means that the species prefers to breed in small bodies of standing water, including fountains, birdbaths, old tires, garbage cans, and even flowerpots (Figure 7.7). These small bodies of water are common in urban and suburban environments. Source reduction by individuals includes elimination of any sources of standing water. These sources must be disposed of or put in places where they do not accumulate water. If the sources cannot be drained, larvicides should be added to the standing water.

Why do *Culex* species prefer to breed in containers? As the standing water begins to evaporate, the nutrients in the water become concentrated. These concentrated nutrients serve as a food source for other organisms. As the water turns into a breeding ground for the bacteria and algae that consume these nutrients, the water also begins to smell bad to humans. To the mosquito, however, the putrid smell signals that the water is full of nutrients that will help its young to grow. The female *Culex* mosquito seeks out these pools of water in which to lay her eggs. By mosquito-proofing your home through the destruction of habitats that encourage mosquito breeding,

Figure 7.7 *Culex* mosquitoes, the species that carries West Nile virus, prefer to breed in small bodies of water. Birdbaths, discarded cups, and even old tires are desirable habitats for these mosquitoes and their larvae. (Centers for Disease Control and Prevention)

you can help prevent adult mosquitoes from spreading the West Nile virus.

People can also avoid mosquito bites by protecting themselves. Measures of self-protection include wearing long-sleeved shirts and long pants to reduce the amount of skin exposed to mosquitoes looking for a meal. You should also avoid going outside, if possible, during prime mosquito-biting hours. When these two preventions are not practical, mosquito repellants should be used. The mosquito repellants that are recommended by the CDC contain DEET (N,N-diethyl-m-toluamide). The pesticide DEET has been used for a long time in the United States, and there is long-term data on its safety. The EPA has deemed DEET to be safe, when used as directed by manufacturers (Figure 7.8). Two scientists have done experiments to determine how long DEET-containing repellents last once they are applied to an individual. From these experiments, it was found that a product containing 100 percent DEET provided up to 12 hours of protection, a product containing 23.8 percent DEET provided up to five hours of protection, while a product containing 6.65 percent DEET provided about two hours of protection.

THE FUTURE OF WEST NILE VIRUS

Since West Nile virus first appeared in the United States in 1999, it has spread through the Western Hemisphere and will inevitably require continuous planning to prevent it from causing devastating economic and health problems. The ongoing surveillance of the virus will help scientists predict when West Nile virus will show up next and where the most likely outbreaks will occur. To some extent, the virus has already chosen certain geographical niches and will likely continue to reappear at those locations year after year. However, the geography of the virus will continue to evolve. If the CDC

Figure 7.8 You can protect yourself from mosquitoes and other insects by using a commercially available insect repellant. The most effective repellants contain the pesticide DEET. (© AP Images)

were able to better understand and predict the forces that drive the dispersal of West Nile virus, then local governments may be able to prepare for upcoming outbreaks.

The CDC has outlined some of the future research that the agency believes will help scientists predict the future spread of West Nile virus. One area of research involves studying the migratory routes of birds in the Western Hemisphere. The virus has been detected in the Caribbean and South America, and was likely spread by these migrating birds.

One important question that remains is whether the virus is able to make a reverse migration when the same birds return. If so, then the virus will have a source of continued replication throughout the winter season. What are the implications for continued year-round replication? This could allow the virus to evolve a broader host range as it is exposed to more species or as the virus becomes more virulent—something scientists are striving to prevent.

The National Institute of Allergy and Infectious Diseases (NIAID) of the National Institutes of Health supports research in many institutions aimed at understanding diseases in humans and animals. One of these diseases is, of course, West Nile virus. Research being funded by the NIAID includes several projects designed to increase understanding of how the virus replicates and spreads through the human body. This area of research will help in the development of vaccines and drugs designed to treat the disease.

Another field of research being funded is that associated with determining which proteins are involved in contributing to the virus's ability to actually cause disease. Knowing this will help to prevent disease, even after a person is infected.

Research aimed at a better understanding of the immune system will help doctors treat the worst form of infection with West Nile virus, West Nile encephalitis. This is very important in helping to reduce the number of deaths associated with this form of the disease.

Funding is also being provided for an examination of the ecology and year-to-year maintenance of mosquito-borne encephalitis viruses and how genetic variation affects the spread and virulence of the virus.

Finally, NIAID is supporting research to study whether migrating bird populations carry the virus to points in Central and South America. This type of spread not only threatens to perpetuate the disease over a much larger geographic area, but helps to increase the number of cases in areas where the birds originated and eventually returned to.

Notes

Chapter 2

1. J. Muzaffar et al., "Dengue Encephalitis: Why We Need to Identify This Entity in a Dengue-prone Region," *Singapore Medical Journal* 47, 11 (2006): 975–977, http://www.ncbi.nlm.nih.gov/pubmed/17075667 (accessed December 12, 2008).
2. Government of Alberta, Canada, "West Nile Virus," *Alberta Health and Wellness* (2008), http://www.health.alberta.ca/public/wnv_history.html (accessed October 9, 2008).
3. G. Huhn et al., "West Nile Virus in the United States: An Update on an Emerging Infectious Disease," *American Family Physician* 68, 4 (2003): 671–672, http://www.aafp.org/afp/20030815/653.html (accessed December 12, 2008).

Chapter 4

1. G. L. Hamer et al., "*Culex pipiens* (Diptera: Culicidae): A Bridge Vector of West Nile Virus to Humans," *Journal of Medical Entomology* 45, no. 1 (2008): 125–128, http://www.ncbi.nlm.nih.gov/pubmed/18283952 (accessed December 12, 2008).
2. K. Padgett et al., "West Nile Virus Infection in Tree Squirrels (Rodentia: Sciuridae) in California, 2004-2005," *American Journal of Tropical Medicine and Hygiene* 76, no. 5 (2007): 810-813, http://www.ajtmh.org/cgi/reprint/76/5/810 (accessed December 12, 2008).
3. Centers for Disease Control and Prevention (CDC), "West Nile Virus Transmission Through Blood Transfusion," *MMWR Morbidity and Mortality Weekly Report* 56, 4 (2007): 76–79, http://www.cdc.gov/mmwr/preview/mmwrhtml/mm5604a4.htm (accessed December 12, 2008).
4. CDC, "Transfusion-Associated Transmission of West Nile Virus—Arizona, 2004," *MMWR Morbidity and Mortality Weekly Report* 53, 36 (2004): 842–844, http://www.cdc.gov/mmwr/preview/mmwrhtml/mm5336a4.htm (accessed December 12, 2008).

Chapter 5

1. A. Perelygin et al., "Positional Cloning of the Murine Flavivirus Resistance Gene," *Proceedings of the National Academy of Science* 99, 14 (2002): 9322–9327, http://www.pnas.org/content/99/14/9322.full.pdf+html (accessed December 12, 2008); T. Mashimo et al., "A Nonsense Mutation in the Gene Encoding 2'-5'-Oligoadenylate Synthetase/L1 Isoform Is Associated With West Nile Virus Susceptibility in Laboratory Mice," *Proceedings of the National Academy of Science* 99, 17 (2002): 11311–11316, http://www.pnas.org/content/99/17/11311.full.pdf+html (accessed December 12, 2008).
2. A. Barrett, "Update on Flavivirus Virulence Studies," Department of Pathology, Center for Tropical Diseases, Sealy Center for Vaccine Development, University of Texas Medical Branch, www.cdc.gov/ncidod/dvbid/westnile/conf/ppt/1b-barret.ppt (accessed September 22, 2008).

Chapter 7

1. RedOrbit.com, "Northern America May Suffer New West Nile Outbreaks," July 4, 2008, http://www.redorbit.com/news/health/1463445/northern_america_may_suffer_new_west_nile_outbreaks/ (accessed on October 8, 2008).
2. CDC, "2008 West Nile Virus Activity in the United States," Statistics, Surveillance and Control, http://www.cdc.gov/ncidod/dvbid/westnile/surv&controlCaseCount08_detailed.htm (accessed on July 7, 2009).
3. Ochs, Ridgely, "The Fight Against West Nile," *Newsday*, September 10, 2008: A2-A3.
4. Harrington, Mark, "How Safe is Scourge?", *Newsday*, September 12, 2008: A8.
5. D. Chang et al., "Single-round Infectious Particles Enhance Immunogenicity of a DNA Vaccine Against West Nile Virus," *Nature Biotechnology* 26 (2008): 571–577, http://www.nature.com/nbt/journal/v26/n5/abs/nbt1400.html (accessed December 12, 2008).

6. S. Powell and K. Ayars, "West Nile Virus Vaccine For Horses Approved; DEM Recommends Protection, Prevention Measures to Farmers and Horse Owners," Rhode Island Department of Environmental Management, August 28, 2001, http://www.dem.ri.gov/news/2001/pr/0828011.htm (accessed on October 9, 2008).

adulticide—A pesticide that destroys an insect in its adult stage.

antibodies—Proteins produced in the blood in response to the presence of a specific antigen. Antibodies recognize and help fight infectious agents and other foreign substances that invade the body.

antigen—Any foreign substance introduced into the body that stimulates an immune response.

apoptosis—A process of cell self-destruction that involves fragmentation of chromosomal DNA and disintegration of the cell into membrane-bound particles that are then eliminated by macrophages.

Arbovirus—An abbreviation for <u>ar</u>thropod-<u>bo</u>rne <u>virus</u>. Any of a large group of viruses transmitted by arthropods that include the causative pathogens of encephalitis.

arthropod—An invertebrate that has jointed limbs and a segmented body with an exoskeleton made of chitin.

asymptomatic—Showing no symptoms of a disease.

attenuated—Reduced or weakened in strength, value, or virulence.

bacterium (plural is *bacteria*)—Any single-celled, prokaryotic microorganism that is free-living.

biosynthesis—The production of a chemical compound by a living organism.

breakbone fever—A common name used for dengue fever because the pain in the bones associated with the disease feels as if they are breaking, although they are not.

chimera—A virus consisting of two or more components of different viruses.

cowpox—A mild contagious skin disease of cattle. When the virus is transmitted to humans, it confers immunity to smallpox, a related virus.

cytoplasm—The part of the cell contained within the cell membrane that may hold the nucleus and/or organelles.

dendritic—Related to the branches of nerve cells (called dendrites) that send signals within the nervous system.

dengue encephalitis—Inflammation of the brain associated with dengue fever, a disease caused by a flavivirus, which is the family of viruses to which West Nile virus belongs.

deoxyribonucleic acid (DNA)—A molecule consisting of two long chains of nucleotides twisted into a double helix and joined by hydrogen bonds between the complementary bases of adenine and thymine or cytosine and guanine. The sequence of the nucleotides determines hereditary characteristics.

encephalitis—Inflammation of the brain.

enzyme-linked immunosorbent assay (ELISA)—A sensitive immunological test that uses an enzyme linked to an antibody as a marker for the detection of a specific antigen. The test is often used to determine if a person or animal has been exposed to a particular infectious agent.

endoplasmic reticulum—System of interconnected cytoplasmic membranes in a cell that plays a role in transporting materials within the cell.

epidemic—An outbreak of a contagious disease that spreads rapidly and widely.

epizootic cycle—The way in which a disease breaks out among animals.

exoskeleton—A hard covering on the outside of the body that provides support and protects the interior bodily tissues.

flavivirus—A family of RNA viruses that are spread by ticks and mosquitoes. Infection by any member of these viruses can potentially cause encephalitis.

hemagglutinin—A protein in a virus that causes red blood cells to clump together.

hemorrhage—Excessive loss of blood from a blood vessel.

host—The single isolated structure that a virus or parasite lives in or on.

incidental host—An organism that is not capable of transmitting a pathogen to another organism. Also called a dead-end host.

larvicide—A pesticide that destroys an insect in its larval stage.

lesions—Tears in the tissue of an organism.

lysis—The death of a cell through an explosion-like process.

meningitis—Inflammation of the meninges, the protective layers of connective tissue that surround the brain and spinal cord. The infection may be caused by bacteria or several different viruses.

meningoencephalitis—Inflammation of both the meninges and the brain. The infection may be caused by protozoans, viruses, or bacteria.

microorganism—A living thing too small to be seen without the aid of a microscope. Examples include bacteria, viruses, and protozoans.

myocarditis—Inflammation of the muscular tissue of the heart.

ornithophilic—Exhibiting a preference for birds.

parasite—An organism that lives in or on another organism, but contributes nothing to the survival of the host.

pathogen—Disease-causing microorganism.

pathogenesis—The development of a disease or death.

pathology—The study of diseases and the changes they cause when they infect someone or something.

replication cycle—The repeated process of creating copies of oneself. In the case of viruses, the process involves entering a cell, creating new virions that leave the cell, and repeating the process.

reservoir—An organism that directly or indirectly spreads a pathogen while being virtually immune to its effects.

ribonucleic acid (RNA)—Molecule consisting of a single long chain of nucleotides. Triplet sequences (three bases) of the nucleotides, or codons, direct the translation of proteins.

ribosome—An organelle located in a cell's cytoplasm that is responsible for making proteins.

serum—The liquid portion of the blood.

smallpox—A highly contagious, often fatal disease that is caused by a poxvirus and characterized by high fever and aches with the eruption of pimples that blister and produce pus.

vaccines—Preparations of antigens that stimulate antibody production or cellular immunity against a pathogen.

vector—An organism that helps spread a pathogen from one organism to another.

viremia—The presence of virus particles in the bloodstream of a host.

virion—A complete viral particle, consisting of the protein shell and nucleic acid genome of the infectious virus.

virulent—Rapidly able to overcome the body's immune defenses and cause disease.

virus—A submicroscopic parasite of plants, animals, and bacteria that often causes disease. Because they are unable to replicate without a host cell, viruses are not considered living organisms.

West Nile poliomyelitis—A condition caused by West Nile virus that resembles poliomyelitis, which is caused by poliovirus. The flaccid paralysis accompanying the condition is similar to that seen in cases of polio and is most likely due to damage to the anterior horn cells of the spinal cord that transmit nerve impulses to muscles.

Bibliography

Anderson, J. F., T. G. Andreadis, et al. "Isolation of West Nile Virus from Mosquitoes, Crows, and a Cooper's Hawk in Connecticut." *Science* 286, no. 5448 (1999): 2331–2333.

Arroyo, J., C. Miller, et al. "ChimeriVax-West Nile Virus Live-attenuated Vaccine: Preclinical Evaluation of Safety, Immunogenicity, and Efficacy." *Journal of Virology* 78, no. 22 (2004): 12497–12507.

Arroyo, J., C. A. Miller, et al. "Yellow Fever Vector Live-virus Vaccines: West Nile Virus Vaccine Development." *Trends in Molecular Medicine* 7, no. 8 (2001): 350–354.

Barrett, A.D.T. "Current Status of Flavivirus Vaccines." *Annals of the New York Academy of Sciences* 951 (2001): 262–271.

Boyce, N. "Travels of a Virus." *U.S. News and World Report* 131, no. 26 (2001): 51.

Brandt, A. L., N. Martyak, et al. "West Nile Virus." *Military Medicine* 169, no. 4 (2004): 261–264.

Bugbee, L. M., and L. R. Forte. "The Discovery of West Nile Virus in Over-wintering *Culex pipiens* (Diptera: Culicidae) Mosquitoes in Lehigh County, Pennsylvania." *Journal of the American Mosquito Control Association* 20, no. 3 (2004): 326–327.

Cunha, B. A. "Differential Diagnosis of West Nile Encephalitis." *Current Opinion in Infectious Diseases* 17, no. 5 (2004): 413–420.

Dean, J. L., and C. P. Schaben. "West Nile Virus: An Overview for the Primary Care Provider." *Current Infectious Disease Reports* 4, no. 4 (2002): 273–275.

Gingrich, J. B., and L. Casillas. "Selected Mosquito Vectors of West Nile Virus: Comparison of Their Ecological Dynamics in Four Woodland and Marsh Habitats in Delaware." *Journal of the American Mosquito Control Association* 20, no. 2 (2004): 138–145.

Granwehr, B. P., K. M. Lillibridge, et al. "West Nile Virus: Where Are We Now?" *The Lancet Infectious Diseases* 4, no. 9 (2004): 547–556.

Guharoy, R., S. A. Gilroy, et al. "West Nile Virus Infection." *American Journal of Health—System Pharmacy* 61, no. 12 (2004): 1235–1241.

Hall, R. A., and A. A. Khromykh. "West Nile Virus Vaccines." *Expert Opinion on Biological Theory* 4, no. 8 (2004): 1295–1305.

Hayes, E. B., and D. R. O'Leary. "West Nile Virus Infection: A Pediatric Perspective." *Pediatrics* 113, no. 5 (2004): 1375–1381.

Henson, G., and P. Hicock. "Rapid Detection of West Nile Virus in Birds Using the VecTest WNV Antigen Assay." *Clinical Laboratory Science* 17, no. 4 (2004): 218–220.

Jia, X. Y., T. Briese, et al. "Genetic Analysis of West Nile New York 1999 Encephalitis Virus." *The Lancet* 354, no. 9194 (1999): 1971–1972.

Kleiboeker, S. B., C. M. Loiacono, et al. "Diagnosis of West Nile Virus Infection in Horses." *Journal of Veterinary Diagnostic Investigation* 16, no. 1 (2004): 2–10.

Knipe, David M., and Peter M. Howley. *Fields Virology*. Philadelphia: Lippincott Williams and Wilkins, 2002.

Kramer, L. D., and K. A. Bernard. "West Nile Virus in the Western Hemisphere." *Current Opinion in Infectious Diseases* 14, no. 5 (2001): 519–525.

Lai, C. J., and T. P. Monath. "Chimeric Flaviviruses: Novel Vaccines Against Dengue Fever, Tick-borne Encephalitis, and Japanese Encephalitis." *Advances in Virus Research* 61 (2003): 469–509.

Lanciotti, R. S., J. T. Roehrig, et al. "Origin of the West Nile Virus Responsible for an Outbreak of Encephalitis in the Northeastern United States." *Science* 286, no. 5448 (1999): 2333–2337.

Lee, J. W., and M. L. Ng. "A Nano-view of West Nile Virus-induced Cellular Changes During Infection." *Journal of Nanobiotechnology* 2, no. 1 (2004): 6.

Malkinson, M., and C. Banet. "The Role of Birds in the Ecology of West Nile Virus in Europe and Africa." *Current Topics in Microbiology and Immunology* 267 (2002): 309–322.

Monath, T. P. "Prospects for Development of a Vaccine Against the West Nile Virus." *Annals of the New York Academy of Sciences* 951 (2001): 1–2.

Morgan, R. "West Nile Viral Encephalitis: A Case Study." *The Journal of Neuroscience Nursing* 36, no. 4 (2004): 185–188.

Muerhoff, A. S., G. J. Dawson, et al. "Enzyme-linked Immunosorbent Assays Using Recombinant Envelope Protein Expressed in COS-1 and Drosophila S2 Cells for Detection of West Nile Virus Immunoglobulin M in Serum or Cerebrospinal Fluid." *Clinical and Diagnostic Laboratory Immunology* 11, no. 4 (2004): 651–657.

"North American Birds and West Nile Virus." *Emerging Infectious Diseases* 10, no. 8 (2004): 1518–1519.

"Outbreak of West Nile–like Viral Encephalitis—New York, 1999." *Morbidity and Mortality Weekly Report* 48, no. 38 (1999): 845–849.

Petersen, L. R., and E. B. Hayes. "Westward Ho?—The Spread of West Nile Virus." *The New England Journal of Medicine* 351, no. 22 (2004): 2257–2259.

Peterson, A. T., D. A. Vieglais, et al. "Migratory Birds Modeled as Critical Transport Agents for West Nile Virus in North America." *Vector Borne and Zoonotic Diseases* 3, no. 1 (2003): 27–37.

Rados, C. "First Test Approved to Help Detect West Nile Virus." *FDA Consumer* 37, no. 5 (2003): 18–19.

Roos, K. L. "West Nile Encephalitis and Myelitis." *Current Opinion in Neurology* 17, no. 3 (2004): 343–346.

Sampson, B. A., and V. Armbrustmacher. "West Nile Encephalitis: The Neuropathology of Four Fatalities." *Annals of the New York Academy of Sciences* 951 (2001): 172–178.

Sejvar, J. J. "West Nile Virus and Poliomyelitis." *Neurology* 63, no. 2 (2004): 206–207.

Sudakin, D. L., and W. R. Trevathan. "DEET: A Review and Update of Safety and Risk in the General Population." *Journal of Toxicology and Clinical Toxicology* 41, no. 6 (2003): 831–839.

Tesh, R. B., R. Parsons, et al. "Year-round West Nile Virus Activity, Gulf Coast Region, Texas and Louisiana." *Emerging Infectious Diseases* 10, no. 9 (2004): 1649–1652.

"Transfusion-associated Transmission of West Nile Virus—Arizona, 2004." *Morbidity and Mortality Weekly Report* 53, no. 36 (2004): 842–844.

Turell, M. J., M. R. Sardelis, et al. "Potential Vectors of West Nile Virus in North America." *Current Topics in Microbiology and Immunology* 267 (2002): 241–252.

"Update: West Nile Virus Screening of Blood Donations and Transfusion-associated Transmission—United States, 2003." *Morbidity and Mortality Weekly Report* 53, no. 13 (2004): 281–284.

"West Nile Virus Activity—United States, November 9–16, 2004." *Morbidity and Mortality Weekly Report* 53, no. 45 (2004): 1071–1072.

White, David O., and Frank J. Fenner. *Medical Virology*. San Diego: Academic Press, 1994.

Yamshchikov, G., V. Borisevich, et al. "An Attenuated West Nile Prototype Virus is Highly Immunogenic and Protects Against the Deadly NY99 Strain: A Candidate for Live WN Vaccine Development." *Virology* 330, no. 1 (2004): 304–312.

Further Resources

Books and Articles

Abramovitz, Melissa. *West Nile Virus.* San Diego: Lucent Books, 2003.

Cann, Alan J. *RNA Viruses: A Practical Approach.* New York: Oxford University Press, 2000.

Goudsmit, Jaap. *Viral Fitness: The Next SARS and West Nile in the Making.* New York: Oxford University Press, 2004.

Knipe, David M., and Peter M. Howley. *Fields Virology.* 5th ed. Philadelphia: Lippincott Williams and Wilkins, 2006.

Margulies, Phillip. *West Nile Virus.* New York: Rosen Publishing, 2003.

White, David O., and Frank J. Fenner. *Medical Virology.* 4th ed. San Diego: Academic Press, 1994.

Web Sites

All the Virology on the WWW
http://www.virology.net/garryfavwebindex.html

Big Picture Book of Viruses
http://www.virology.net/Big_Virology/BVHomePage.html

Centers for Disease Control (CDC),
Division of Vector-Borne Infectious Diseases, West Nile Virus
http://www.cdc.gov/ncidod/dvbid/westnile

CNN.com Health Library, West Nile Virus
http://www.cnn.com/HEALTH/library/west-nile-virus/DS00435.html

Environmental Health Perspectives Online
http://www.ehponline.org

Morbidity and Mortality Weekly Report
http://www.cdc.gov/mmwr/index.html

U.S. Geological Survey, West Nile Virus Maps
http://westnilemaps.usgs.gov

Chamberland, Charles, 32
Chamberland filter, 32
Chamberland-Pasteur filter, 32
children, 75
chimera, 91–93, *92*
ChimeriVax, 91–93
coagulation, and mosquito bite, 58–60, *59*
communicable diseases, 6–7
container breeders, mosquitoes as, 54–55, 85, 101–102, *102*
Corvidae (crows), 42–43, 51–52, 95–96
Corvus corone (hooded crow), 51–52
cowpox, 86
C protein. *See* capsid protein
Crick, Francis, 34
crows, 42–43, 51–52, 95–96
Culex mosquitoes, 17–18, *46*, 46–48, 54–56, 85, 100
cytoplasm, 38

DDT, 89
dead-end host, 45–46, 55
DEET, 102–103, *103*
dendritic cells, 60
dengue encephalitis, 17
dengue fever, 17–18, 21*t*
deoxyribonucleic acid (DNA), 34
diagnosis, 76–82
DNA. *See* deoxyribonucleic acid

DNA sequencing
  of mosquito blood meals, 46–48
  of West Nile virus, 82
DNA vaccines, 93–94
eastern gray squirrel, 52
Egypt, 20
electron microscopy, *30*, 33, 39, 80–82, *81*
ELISA. *See* enzyme-linked immunosorbent assay
emerging infections, 6
encephalitis
  Australian X disease, 18–19
  definition of, 10, 23
  dengue, 17
  diagnosis of, 76–77
  fatal, 72–75
  olfactory route for, 63–65
  pathogenesis of, 13, 62–66, 72–75
  poliovirus, 13
  rabies, 13
  St. Louis, 19
  subclinical, 72–75
  symptoms of, 23
  West Nile, 10
    blood-brain barrier and, 62–66, *63*
    New York City outbreak of, 20–23
    patterns of pathogenesis, 72–75
endoplasmic reticulum, 66
entry of virus, in U.S., 25–27, *26*
envelope (E) protein, 30–31, *31*, 34–35, *36*, 40, 92

Environmental Protection Agency (EPA), 89, 102
enzyme-linked immunosorbent assay (ELISA), 47, 78–80, *79*
EPA. *See* Environmental Protection Agency
epidemic, 43
epizootic cycle, 97
E protein. *See* envelope protein
evolution of viruses, 75
exoskeleton, 14

fatal encephalitis, 72–75, 83
feeding by mosquitoes, 46–48, 54–55, 57–58, 94
Flaviviridae, 13–20, 21*t*
flavivirus, 16–20
Fort Dodge Laboratories, 84, 94
fox squirrel, 52, *53*
France, 20
future, of West Nile virus, 103–105

gene gun, 93, 95
genetic sequencing
  of mosquito blood meals, 46–48
  of West Nile virus, 82
genetic susceptibility, 65, 74
genome
  evolution of, 75
  of virus, 34
  of West Nile virus, replication of, 35–38
glossary, 108–111

and St. Louis encepha-
litis, 19
in urban environment,
54–55, 85
and West Nile virus, 11,
42–56
Culex carriers, 17–18,
46, 46–48, 54–56
feeding habits (blood
meals) and, 46–48,
54–55, 57–58, 94
as mode of entry in
U.S., 25–26
as vector, *44,* 45–46,
48, 54–56
viremia and, 48–52,
51
and yellow fever, 17
mosquito repellants,
102–103, *103*
mother-to-child trans-
mission, 54
M protein. *See* mem-
brane protein
Murray Valley encephali-
tis virus, 19
myocarditis, 24

National Institute of
Allergy and Infectious
Diseases (NIAID),
104–105
National Institutes
of Health (NIH),
104–105
National Veterinary
Services Laboratory
(NVSL), 24, 80
New York City, 20–23,
77–78, 80, 82, 95–96
NIAID. *See* National
Institute of Allergy
and Infectious
Diseases

NIH. *See* National
Institutes of Health
nonstructural proteins,
of West Nile virus,
31–32, 39–40
no risk category, 96
nucleocapsid, 40
NVSL. *See* National
Veterinary Services
Laboratory

olfactory route, for
encephalitis, 63–65
online resources, 116
organophosphate, 98
organ transplantation,
and virus transmis-
sion, 54
ornithophilic, definition
of, 54

pandemics, 6
panic (1999), 8–12, 43
parasite, 50
passaging, in vaccine
development, 89–91,
91
pathogenesis
of encephalitis, 13
patterns of, 72–75
of West Nile virus,
57–75
pathogens, 13
pathology, 72
Pawan, Joseph Lennox,
13
PCR. *See* polymerase
chain reaction
pesticides, 88–89, 96–101
phagocytosis, 67–69, *68*
Phipps, James, 86
piperonyl butoxide, 88
pKUNdC/C vaccine,
93–94

Plasmodium, 50
poliomyelitis, West Nile,
10
poliovirus encephalitis,
13
polyhedron, 40
polymerase chain reac-
tion (PCR), in mos-
quito blood meals,
46–48
polyprotein, 38
PreveNile, 91
prevention
human self-protection,
102–103
mosquito control/
elimination, 88–89,
96–101
source reduction,
100–103, *102*
vaccines, 11, 84–94
proboscis, of mosquito,
59, *59*
programmed cell death,
67–72, *68, 69*
protein(s), of West Nile
virus
capsid (C), 30–32, *31,*
38–39, 40
envelope (E), 30–31,
31, 34–35, 36, 40, 92
matrix/membrane (M),
30–32, *31,* 39, 40, 92
nonstructural, 31–32,
39–40
structural, 30–32, *31,*
38–39
synthesis of new, 38–40
public alerts, 97

rabies encephalitis, 13
receptors, for West Nile
virus, 34–35
Reed, Walter, *16,* 16–17

About the Author

Dr. Alan I. Hecht is a practicing chiropractor in New York. He is also an adjunct professor at Farmingdale State College and Nassau Community College and an adjunct associate professor at the C.W. Post campus of Long Island University. He teaches courses in medical microbiology, anatomy and physiology, comparative anatomy, human physiology, embryology, and general biology. In addition, he is the course coordinator for Human Biology at Hofstra University where he is an adjunct assistant professor.

Dr. Hecht received his B.S. in Biology–Pre-Medical Studies from Fairleigh Dickinson University in Teaneck, New Jerset. He received his M.S. in Basic Medical Sciences from New York University School of Medicine. He also received his Doctor of Chiropractic (D.C.) degree from New York Chiropractic College in Brookville, New York.

About the Consulting Editor

Hilary Babcock, M.D., M.P.H., is an assistant professor of Medicine at Washington University School of Medicine at Washington University School of Medicine and the Medical Director of Occupational Health for Barnes-Jewish Hospital and St. Louis Children's Hospital. She received her undergraduate degree from Brown University and her M.D. from the University of Texas Southwestern Medical Center at Dallas. After completing her residency, chief residency, and Infectious Disease fellowship at Barnes-Jewish Hospital, she joined the faculty of the Infectious Disease division. She completed an M.P.H. in Public Health from St. Louis University School of Public Health in 2006. She has lectured, taught, and written extensively about infectious diseases, their treatment, and their prevention. She is a member of numerous medical associations and is board certified in infectious disease. She lives in St. Louis, Missouri.